New Orleans

Ghosts II

Victor C. Klein

ISBN 0-9661812-2-0

Library of Congress Catalog Card Number

Design Production: Victor C. Klein

Published by Lycanthrope Press
PO Box 9028
Metairie, LA 70005-9028
L. Talbot, Senor Editor
(504) 866-9756

All proceeds from the sale of this work are the exclusive property of Ordo Templi Veritatis and are used to advance its metaphysickal researches and purposes.

Dedication

To Caroline Albritton and Wolfgang
who now embrace the spirits

Table of Contents

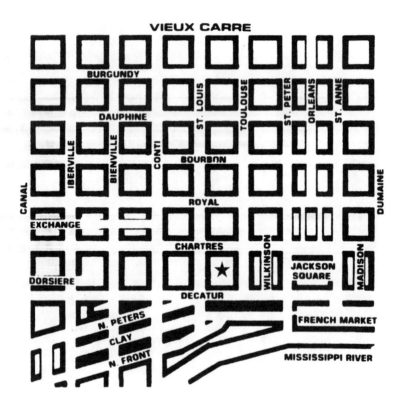

Introduction

Autumn, 1957, my mother kept me home from school. I was ill. Daytime TV offered me no comfort. In those days New Orleans had only two channels, both featuring mindless, dreadful *Soap Operas*. In order to pass the time on that cool, fall day I decided to peruse my mother's library. It was a fateful decision. My eye fell upon *Ghost Stories of Old New Orleans*, by Jeanne de Lavigne. I read all forty stories, three hundred seventy-five pages, during my two day illness. Some thirty-five years later that book would forever change my life.

Thirty-five years saw dramatic changes and events that shaped my life. I earned five university degrees. I fell in and out of love, fathered children and pursued varied careers in academia, government and sales. As middle age approached I was unfulfilled and unhappy. It was during this time, in the forty-first year of my existence, that I suffered an accident which resulted in my being confined to my bed for almost six months. Reflecting upon my life I realized that had my accident cost me my life that life could be judiciously summed on my tombstone. The thought of my life's being bequeathed to posterity as simply a name and two dates created an angst that tore at my soul as a deamon's talon. I languished in my subjective hell rebelling against my historical insignificance.

Aperçu. Satori. Enlightenment. In my fear-filled room I found the key to bring meaning to my life. I remembered that long ago autumn day when I stumbled upon de Lavigne's fascinating tome. I found the work. I re-read it. Here was my plan. Using her book as a primary source I would create my own work and leave posterity the fruits of my labor.

I have always been enamored with books, literature, authors. One of my university degrees is a Master of Library Science granted by Louisiana State University in Baton Rouge (1986). Applying the knowledge and skills I acquired in the pursuit of this degree I examined de Lavigne's book with the critical eye of a scholar/librarian.   Her book, while remarkably readable, entertaining and informative, lacked certain essentials that would qualify it as an anthropologically significant effort. She had no bibliography, footnotes nor index. Her illustrations were limited to pen and ink drawings which were dramatic but few. Also, it was difficult to locate the sites she described because she gave few addresses and only sketchy descriptions of the locales of which she writes. I incorporated these critiques into the body of my work *New Orleans Ghosts.* I have one hundred thirty-one footnotes, thirty-five elements comprising the bibliography and one hundred eighteen entries in the index. The table of contents lists all of the addresses of the sites discussed in the text.   Illustrations include a map of the Vieux Carré (French Quarter), Marie Laveau's death certificate and sixteen photographs. It should also be mentioned that *New Orleans Ghosts* is the only work written exclusively about the ghosts of New Orleans since de Lavigne's 1946 publication.

After three plus years of research, rewrites, investigations and interviews, I submitted my efforts to a literary agent. He liked my product, but offered a series of *suggestions* that consumed another year to incorporate. Finally, four and a half years and three typists later, he began to push my manuscript. Six more months passed before he informed me that no publisher was interested in my creation. I now quote from one of the rejection letters he received which sums up essentially the content of the dozen or so letters he entertained on my behalf.

We are in receipt of Mr. Klein's manuscript New Orleans Ghosts. It is a great idea which is well written and formatted. *His stories are well documented, succinct and fast paced. The MS. held my attention from beginning to end.*

Unfortunately, we are not able to publish New Orleans Ghosts at this time. This is Mr. Klein's first effort and he has not established economic viability. Once he can demonstrate that his works sell we will be more than happy to publish him . . . .

Catch 22; I was devastated. I have faith in nothing but my abilities and my art. As a consequence of this I elected to self publish. Almost five years after this decision I am the best selling, self published author in the Gulf South! Not only am I an author, but I am CEO of my own publishing company Lycanthrope Press. *New Orleans Ghosts* is such a resounding success that I have been encouraged to create a sequel *New Orleans Ghosts II*. This present work is modeled after the first. The only changes I have incorporated are that the footnotes are included in the text and do not appear as a separate chapter. Also I have attached several appendices in order that the serious reader may benefit from my historical research. I feel that this documentation should be preserved. With this sequel the reader can enjoy forty-four chapters that will transport her on a mystical journey of fact filled terror that is both entertaining and enlightening.

Before the appearance of *New Orleans Ghosts* there were no ghost tours in the city. Since the publication of my work over a dozen ghost tours have come into existence using my book as their basis. The book has provided employment to some and entertainment for tens of thousands. It is a dynamic contribution to the city's second largest industry–Tourism. My life has made a difference to history. I am proud to have contributed to my city; made a significant contribution to the existing body of recorded knowledge; become a successful author; and justified my existence. My life is fulfilled and fulfilling. I now consider myself to be a human being of some historical significance. I have an identity, an identity that has granted me immortality.

House Guests

Two industries drive the economic engine of The Big Easy: the port and tourism. Annually, the port accommodates an average of 4,000 vessel calls. In 1997 Metrovision survey recorded the port employed 19,850, 18% of the work force, with annual revenues of $573 million.

Each year New Orleans' 181square miles and approximately half a million residents play host to 3.7 million Mardi Gras revelers, 455,000+ Jazz Fest affectionados, 250,000+ French Quarter Festival fans, 160,000 black heritage and Essence Music Festival devotees, and over 2.5 million others who come for athletic spectacles, concerts and fairs, not to mention just plain vacationers, according to New Orleans Convention and Visitors Bureau statistics.

Hotels play a vital role in the city's economic well being. This beginning chapter is addressed to all of you who would like a little something *extra* with your accommodations. The following list of thirteen (13) hotels should be enough to whet the palates of those who entertain the possibility of an encounter of an unknown kind.

Note: The hotels are arranged alphabetically. All of the streets in the French Quarter are designated as *rue*. This is the traditional French manner of designating streets.

Addresses and phone numbers are included as well as the average price for double occupancy. Material for Le Pavillion and Park View was gathered by the author through interviews and personal investigations. All of the other stories were surfaced from *Journey into Darkness*, by Katherine Smith (pp. 51-63). These sites were further explored by visitations and/or interviews by the author.

Andrew Jackson Hotel
($70 - $139)
919 rue Royal
(504) 561-5881
70116

It has been reported that the ghost of Andrew Jackson has made varied appearances; however, his ghost is only fleeting.

In 1794, the site was occupied by a boys' boarding school. When fire ravaged the city that night five youths lost their lives in the inferno. The most pregnant haunting involves these lost little souls. The hotel is an *adults-only* establishment. Despite this fact, there are numerous complaints about boisterous children.   Sounds of laughter, singing, talking, yelling, screaming, gasping have long belabored guests and staff alike.

Bourbon Orleans Hotel
($250 and up)
717 rue Orleans
(504) 523-2222
70116

Rebuilt in 1871, this site was always the center of fun and frivorality. After the Battle of New Orleans (18 January1814), Andrew Jackson announced his intention to seek the presidency of the United States at a ball held here. Parties, liquor, sex, gambling were no strangers at these doors.

By 1870, things had quieted down considerably. The Sisters of the Holy Family operated a convent and an orphanage for *enfants de couleur* (children of color). Here they remained until 1963 when it was acquired as a hotel.

The Bourbon Orleans is not only one of the finest in the world, but also probably the most haunted. Enjoy a breakfast of Eggs Hollandaise and Bloody Marys. Then look around for any of the many hauntings that have been reported, but watch your language for the old nuns might take offense and slap you in the chops.

In the ballroom ladies may be surprised by the advances of a dashing young creole who kisses necks and caresses cheeks. The fifth floor is home to a beautiful blond girl who chases her ectoplasmic ball through halls and walls. Be careful of the sixth floor. Water faucets have a predilection to turn themselves on. The seventh floor is patrolled by a benign, old Confederate soldier who parades about with his rifle on his shoulder.

Creole House
($130)
1013 rue St. Ann
(504) 524-8076
70116

Once owned by Marie Laveau (see *New Orleans Ghosts*, Klein, 1996), this property has been baptized by Voo-Doo and witchcraft. Hauntings seem to center around doors and doorways. Could this be some Occult metaphor?

Lafitte Guest House
($119 - $199)
1003 rue Bourbon
(504) 581-2678
70116

When this was a private home intense tragedy burned into what would become Room 21. A mourning mother bewails the loss of her two daughters. One falls to yellow fever. Her distraught daughter surrenders to the rope and stool.

LePavillon
($95 - $230)
833 Poydras Street
(504) 581-3111
70112

During the colonial period (1718 - 1803) the land upon which this gorgeous hotel sits was soaked in blood. It was a mosquito and serpent-infested swamp that held whorehouses, bawdy bars, opium dens and unnumbered murder victims. The area was the preferred option for the disposal of unwanted corpses. Robbery victims, prostitutes, scorned lovers, suicides all crossed the River Styx from this location.

On several booksigning occasions the author has met guests of the hotel who have alleged spiritual manifestations. Requests for an interview have been ignored.

Le Richelieu Hotel
($130)
1234 rue Chartres
(504) 529-2492
70116

In 1802 several Spanish soldiers were executed in what was to become the courtyard of the present hotel. Various witnesses have reported seeing ghostly soldiers.

Olivier House
($125)
828 rue Toulouse
(504) 525-8456
70112

Ensconced in these walls is a classic ghost story. An old woman dressed in black rambles around ceaselessly reciting her rosary, occasionally cursing and screaming at those who interrupt her devotions.

Researchers believe the ghost is that of Madame Elizabeth Duparc Locoul (1796 - 1884). She acquired the property, erected in 1836, from Madame Olivier, a prosperous plantation owner and socialite. Madame Locoul was a devout Catholic who continually recited the Rosary, beat and berated her slaves and was such a miser that after her death it was discovered she had preserved her baby teeth. It is alleged that her presence in the first room of the hotel is especially strong.

Omni Royal Orleans Hotel
($169 - $239)
621 rue St. Louis
(504) 529-5333
70130

In ante-bellum times a slave exchange stood here. Not withstanding, the negativity of such activity has no relevance to the present day haunting. At the turn of the nineteenth century the finer hotels upheld a charming tradition. On cold nights, a maid could be summoned to warm one's bed. This was accomplished by the maid's placing copper pans filled with hot coals on the mattress. She would then "tuck in" the guest snugly by pushing the cover's ends under the mattress. That service faded with the previous century; however, it is kept alive by a benevolent spirit who, on occasion, comforts some fortunate guests at this fabulous hotel.

Park View Guest House
($119 w/bath; $109 w/o bath)
7004 St. Charles Avenue
(504) 861-7564
70118

This elegant guest house was built to accommodate tourists who flocked to the city for the World's Fair and Cotton Centennial Exposition opening 16 December 1884. The Fair boasted the largest conservatory in the world, the 116,400 square-foot Horticultural Hall (Huber, p. 240).

This site came to the author's attention by one Carlos, former manager of the hotel. He alleged that, he, several guests, and staff experienced eerie happenings associated with Room 17. The author lives one block from the hotel so Carlos and his wife were frequently seen in the neighborhood (they lived on the premises). Carlos and I talked about many subjects. When we spoke of my books or my interest in the paranormal he would update me about Room 17. Key missing. Door unlocked. Water on floor.

One night while walking my German Shepard Dog Wolfgang he called me to his porch and introduced me to a guest from Los

Angeles. The gentleman was involved in media production. He was a large man (6'5", 275+ lbs.), well spoken and intelligent.

He related the following:

> *. . . about 4:00 a.m.. I woke up because the foot of the bed was being lifted. My first thought was – Earthquake! Then I realized I was in New Orleans. The damn bed was a good 18 inches off the floor. I looked at my wife. She was staring at the foot of the bed. There was a shadow or something at the edge of the bed. I lunged at him or whatever. There was nothing there.*

My advice is book Room 17 at least a year in advance.

Place d'Armes Hotel
($120 - $170)
625 rue St. Ann
(504) 524-4531
70116

There are substantial allegations that this inn has a panoply of ghostly manifestations. One is an educated, bearded man who is supposed to be the ghost of a victim of the great fire of 1788. After the fire the Spanish occupied the site with a jail and gallows.

The ghost of a child plays across the boundary of life and death with a rubber ball, as well as a variety of electrical phenomena.

Provincial Hotel
($99 and up)
1024 rue Chartres
(504) 581-4995
70116

During the war of the Great Rebellion, this edifice was a hospital for Confederate soldiers. Building 5 of the present-day hotel was a ward for critically maimed or ill men. Not surprisingly this building is the only part of the hotel alleged to be haunted. Staff have reported encounters with phantom soldiers in grey, blood stains that come and go, and spectral surgeons gingerly removing arms and legs. Bring a camera and fast ASA (1000) 35mm film and you may bag a boogie man.

Ramada Hotel
($99.00)
1732 Canal Street
(504) 412-4000
70112

Allegations of electrical anomalies as well as "... *misty, dancing apparition* ..." (Smith, p. 52) have been voiced.

Villa Covento Guest House
($89)
616 rue Ursulines
(504) 522-1793
70116

Dating from the 1840's this comfortable guest house holds the laughter of children on the fourth floor. Room 209 has electrical blackouts, and a former guest reported supernatural happenings in Room 120. Sounds like a fun place!

Park View Guest House

The Devil's Mansion

Madeleine Frenau was a sensual, beautiful young woman with desires as exotic as her porcelain body (de Lavigne, p. 117).

She participated in the city's Voo-Doo rituals. The dances of the swamp witches brought her excitement and exhaustion. Her ears heard tales of the Cathari and Bogomils whom Pope Innocent III (R.1198-1216) burned alive for their blasphemes. Madeleine's supple, yielding body thrived on pleasure. Her quick, dark mind thirsted for knowledge.

Somewhere in her quest she met Him! Power flowed from his pitch-like eyes. His manner was commanding, elegant. In perfect Parisian French he promised, "I shall take you places you've never been. I shall show you things you've never seen; then I shall consume you with exquisite passion."

They disappeared together down the velvet, black road. She fell into his embrace, and into the void. She knew the desire embibed by Eve. Madeleine became Lucifer's lover. Their affair brought her rare jewels. Her wardrobe rivaled that of any monarch. Liquors, wines, drugs, tonics and exquisite culinary delicacies all filled her spare time. After all, the Devil is a very busy, but generous man. She had virtually anything she wished except a mansion from which to reign. As they embraced she told him of her desire for a house–a home. She felt him penetrate her farther than she thought safe. Her insides quivered then exploded in a sea of his steaming semen. His laughter caused the clouds to weep.

"Why, yes my sweet carbunkel," he replied. "I'll even build it myself. It shall mirror your soul and my love."

Hobbs decided upon an address in the American sector of the city–1301 Saint Charles Avenue.   Old Pip is an eccentric architect, and his creation showed it. To begin with he built each room separately as a thing in and of itself. The house was constructed room by room.   It seemed as if he was using building blocks rather than a foundation, frame, roof, etc. As a result of his peculiar construction methods no right angle existed in his den. No floor was level. No door was squared. The rarest of woods, and the finest of crystal, marble, limestone pulled form from the air.   The house, while magnificent, disturbed the senses so that passers by averted their eyes. Gargoyles and inverted angles guarded cornices and gables. Ebony paint and gold foil further wrapped the structure in secrecy, silence and splendor.

It seems as though Leviathan taught his paramour too well. She learned of sensuality and love as well as betrayal. While her dark prince labored on their abode she found a human lover as an appetizer.

Alcide Cancienne was every inch the Chevalier of 1840's New Orleans. He was long of limb with a barreling to his chest. His Creole ancestry was displayed by sea green eyes and luxuriant dark hair. Riding, fencing, marksmanship as well as absinthe, octoroon balls and gaming occupied his time in the Queen City of the South.

Their eyes first met in St. Louis Cemetery I.   He was mourning his sister. She prowled for passion. Never had he met such a woman. No caress, no embrace did she deny. They loved for hours. Dawn shattered the night when she said to him, *Alcide, my lovely Alcide, let me take you places you've never been and show you things you've never seen.*

As he gazed on her flawless body she slightly pierced her left breast with a talon like, coral-red nail.

At the moment of our orgasm, my love, drink of my blood, for when you do you shall see my life, my soul, my desires and oh, yes, my dear, my dread.

When the moment came they exchanged fluids. Alcide's body and mind exploded into indescribable ecstasies. At once he became her. The sum total of all of her pleasures and memories became his as his body melted into hers. These were passions unmeant for human experience. Each second was a universe unfolding arcane dimensions of fulfillment. Not only did she share her pleasures with him, she also bequeathed him her terrors. He understood totally her identity and her commitment.

Soon the mansion was completed. Her happiness was complete. The chaotic geometry of Madeleine's lair added to her joy. It exerted a morphic field which continually stimulated everyday events into spectacles of grandeur. Lovemaking with her Satanic Savior transcended blood and semen and drove into realms which have no correspondence in scant four dimensions. Her passions were further exacerbated by the knowledge that she would soon teach these practices to Alcide. Student and teacher, mistress and master. Soon the Tao of experience would be hers to command.

When Legion left Alcide came. Apart from making love Alcide was her companion at the lavish masques and suppers she orchestrated. She sat at the head of a great dining table heavy with a service of pure gold. Before her unfolded a gallery of delights to be shared by her, Alcide and their couture of guests. When not in Baal's arms or Alcide's she reveled with her social life. Among her companions at her frequent banquets were such notables as Rape, Incest, Sodomy, Analingus and her twin brother Cunnilingus is escorted by Monsieur Fallatio. Cannibalism and his dark soul mate, Necrophilia, always added gaiety to the ensemble. Mlle. Paraphilia had eyes for Monsieur Aldice, while Baron Coprophilia hungered for Mme. Madeleine. Her parties were interesting affairs.

One night in the midst of frivolity, Alcide's mind snapped like a hangman's botched knot. He knew for every second of pleasure he savored a millennium of torture awaited him.

You fuckin bitch! You've stolen my soul! My soul, my soul, oh, dear God, forgive me, Forgive me . . ., his words were shattered into silence by the voice of his lover, *You miserable, festering worm. I look forward to sodomizing your miserable ass in Hell.*

Rage shattered his throat. That same rage embraced his disgruntled hostess. Alcide flew at Madeleine seeking Prince Murder. The Prince awaited his arrival as the claw of his beloved. In an instant her hand slashed into his chest lacerating his pectoralis major in four smooth flowing rivers of red revealing the white, bedrock bone below.

His body fell heavy on the lavish table. Rage relinquished his embrace to the hot breath of Madame Fear. Alcide's clouded eyes beheld Mlle. Frenau's lithe, white body descending upon him. Her nails penetrated his clavicles as her fingers crumpled his shoulder joints. In an instant Marquise Pain joined Madam Fear's congress. The Scarlet Harlot tore his pants from his bleeding belly with her razor-sharp toenails. She released her grip in order to present him with a blow that shattered his jaw. His head snapped back to pour blood on the fine Irish lace that merrily covered the sumptuous, formal table.

From fear filled eyes he saw her rise above him. The pain retreated. For a brief second he thought he was free to go. To go seek forgiveness from a God whom he knew was forgiving and merciful. To holy mother church to cleanse him from his most mortal sins. To Jesus who would once again love him. His goals for salvation exploded as Madeleine's fangs excised his genitalia. Terror and Hopelessness joined the orgy. Alcide was overjoyed when Death fell into the company.

Slowly, hostess and guests regained their decorum. Pleasantries were exchanged and complements traded. The party continued along its rosy path.

It began imperceptively. A miasmic effluvia descended in labored breaths over the happy group. Soon they all felt its dreadful, demanding presence. The guests streamed from the house leaving the beautiful, blood splattered Madeleine to have her lover alone.

Help me! This man . . . he . . . he tried to kill me! she pleaded.

Why, my pet, you've certainly made a grand mess of this sorry sack of shit, but you didn't finish your task, he cooed in a husky whisper.

He grabbed her hair and her dead lover's throat and ascended to the attic. This was His domain. She never entered this realm. Within the attic was a cacophony of sounds, smells, sights.   On one wall she witnessed her shared passion with Alcide. Another wall projected her sordid sex with this world's Prince. All of the events of her life cascaded before her as orgasms shook her alabaster body. Through heavy lids she watched as the Creole gentleman's form was devoured with repulsive haste. The Devil turned to her to present his reeking anus. Amid a thunder of gas Alcide's skin oozed out of the stinking orifice. It inflated as some ghastly balloon and floated toward the ceiling. A dozen or so cats paraded below the bloated husk screeching and fighting for the tid-bits that dripped from the grotesque skin (Ibid, p. 11).

Now, Ole' Pip turned his interest toward Mme. She could not resist. His penis slid smoothly into her yielding vagina. A hot tongue probed her salivating mouth.   The mere physical organism gave way to the waves with spiritual climax that only Satan could dispense. She was abandoned to a cyclone of experience and pleasure that defined her in terms of divinity–Apotheosis. Every cell of her being was encased in his lust. Lucifer withdrew from her embrace. Below the shadow of his flaccid member was the equally flaccid skins of Madeleine. The felines fell upon this bounty reducing her remains to a moist slick.

After several days the neighbors recognized her absence. The authorities entered a bare-boned, immaculate house. No furniture. No dust. No fixtures. No spiders. All that remained to remind one that once there was life behind those doors was the lingering smell of death.

For years The Devil's Mansion lay fallow. It loomed in the forbidding darkness of night. By day it radiated mold and grime. The fountain, with its erotic figures, was strangled by thorny weeds. Heavy planks covered the windows; chains barred the doors.

After several decades a succession of tenants occupied the house. Each had short tenure. What drove them away was the nightly appearance of a ghostly dining table. It was set for two in the finest service. Madeleine and Alcide materialized to begin their supper from hell. Soon their tastes transcended their meal. The couple begin a series of embraces that would shock a Basin Street crib whore. By the time their revelries ceased, the room was awash with ectoplasmic viscera and blood.   Then everything vanished. The room returned to normal. The witnessing family fled in panic.

Such was the home's history until Laura Beauregard Larendon and her husband, Charles B. Larendon, took occupancy. Madam Larendon could boast General Pierre Gustave Toutant-Beauregard as her father. The couple spent happy years here. A daughter came, and so did the death of Laura.

Charles was inconsolable. He traveled with his tiny child to Atlanta. There he entrusted her with loving relations. Returning to the St. Charles Avenue address, he began his career as a recluse. Disrepair again covered the edifice. Monsieur Larendon's neighbors forgot his face. There he remained among the ghosts and his memories until death evicted him.

The house remained empty until it was demolished in 1930. A succession of buildings paraded across the lot. Today the land boasts a recently constructed fast food outlet. All that remains to remind us of that eldritch structure are the notes and diaries Charles compiled in his feverish days and tormented nights within its walls. It is he who has preserved this legacy with his solitary writings (Ibid).

Mona Lisa

N ew Orleans City Park encompasses over 1,400 acres of bayous, marsh, ancient oaks and strange history. The area was first inhabited by Native Americans who took advantage of its unique geography. An Indian village arose here and was a center for trade. Located on Bayou St. John and Lake Pontchartrain, it is linked to the Mississippi by a rise of land called Metairie Ridge. The village formed a natural link between the lake and the river. The village was so prosperous and well located that it established early, but devastating contact with the original French settlers (Ryan, p. 1).

Smallpox, measles, war, slavery, genocide obliterated the community. By circa 1740 a young French officer, Chevalier d'Aubant, disappointed in love, fled to the Louisiana colony and retired to the deserted village. There among the ghosts of the Choctaw he built a crude hut. He lived off the land and lake. He lived apart from his own kind. When he finally died his lodge was explored.

In his dwelling hung a portrait of a beautiful female. On a table beneath it lay a crown resting, not on a cushion, but on a heart which it crushed with its weight, and at which the lady gazed with intense melancholy (Ryan, p. 2).

Circa 1800 that acreage and more became a plantation controlled by the three Allard brothers (Wellborn, p. 3). The suffering and death of the Native Americans were replaced by that of the Negro slave. It is from the stewardship of Robert Allard that the present legend allegedly germinates. It is a tale heard by generations of New Orleans' young and horny. I will relate the story as it was told to me when I was a horny high school kid (1961ff) on the prowl for places to *Make Out*. The boy who told it to me, Leo Favalora, is dead.

Seems there's a stretch of road surrounded on one side by woods, and on the other side a mosquito and alligator-infested bayou. It has no light. Dark. Secretive. Potentially dangerous. For a long time and ever since romantic couples enjoyed the embrace of the silent road. Every so often something happens, like what happened three or four years ago. It was in the papers and everything. This will scare the shit out of you and maybe even worse.

Well, here it is. There was a dude from Nicholls High School and his chick who used to come out here real regular, like almost the whole weekend. They came out here so much that she was knocked up by almost four months so the autopsy figured. He was seventeen, and she was fifteen.

One night they were out there really gettin' it on. The still shadows began to wail. Not loud at first but building from a soft sigh to a screech of slander. They pulled from their dripping embrace; eyes and ears straining for clues. Inside their passion mobile the temperature dropped thirty degrees. Each breath was measured as clouds of vapor. Before them through the windshield came a luminous white light. As they held each other in terror, the light transformed into the figure of a slim, brunette speeding toward them. Her mouth was a gaping black hole framed from above by burning red eyes. The frigid car filled with the smell of death. In fear he gripped the car seat when his fingers hit the tire iron he always kept by the door. It was probably more testosterone than courage, but he flew out of the car yellin', "C'mon, Motha Fuckah, ya wanna piece of ma' ass? Fuck Yooou!"

His pregnant girlfriend screamed in vain. He swung wildly at the apparition, so wildly that he fell into the putrid sludge of the Bayou. The fall broke his right arm and ankle. He had a concussion. When they found him the next morning, ravaged by insect bites and exposure, he was in a babbling coma. Part of his babble consisted of repeating Mona, Mona Lisa, Lisa, then a scream. He's still like that today. They got him up at Jackson State Hospital for the criminally insane. You see they found his girlfriend about ten yards from the truck in the woods–Dead! She had taken one hell of a beating. Spatters of blood marked the beginning of the trail which ended with her bruised, lacerated, naked body. The fetus, still attached by the umbilical cord lay about two feet from the rear of her ass. Its little head had been crushed by powerful, yet delicate hands. The coroner said you could see the finger marks in the soft, battered skull.

The cops were nervous. In order to close the case they just blamed it on boyfriend. They figured she demanded he do something about her pregnancy, their baby. He snapped. Raped her. They found semen in her snatch. He beat her to death. He went insane. Since he was a blithering idiot with no chance of recovery, justice sentenced him to life in a hospital for the hopeless, criminally insane. Of course, everybody knows it's a cover up since that shit has been going on out there for about a hundred years. My grandpa said he heard tell of a boy . . . .

Upon investigating this event the author gained additional data. The spectre is alleged to be the daughter of Monsieur Allard, the owner of the plantation during the time of the Civil

Mona Lisa's Road

War.   His daughter Lisa was in love with a dashing, young Confederate Officer. Their passion was unabashed. They loved beyond the boundaries of *decency*. Her father, aghast at the liberties taken with his daughter, forbade the young man from further contact. Their engagement was off. The young officer was escorted from the plantation by two overseers and a burly Negro slave.

Lisa cried. *No,* she moaned.

Not only was her love gone, but now her honor would be vanquished. She was pregnant. Under such duress her father stopped her moaning by acquiescing to a hasty marriage and a long honeymoon–not unusual for genteel couples who found themselves in the *desperation of love*.

Before the bands could be posted, the brave, young, heartbroken soldier fell on the field of valor at Vicksburg. She moaned when she received the letter. She moaned throughout her pregnancy. One tear stained night she ran moaning from the stately plantation. The next morning her unhappy body was found on the road.   Her miscarriage caused massive hemorrhaging.

Such is the story, with variations, that has been handed down to generations of New Orleans' sons and daughters. During the investigation of this event several facts became apparent:

1) Robert Allard died in 1824. He is buried on the plantation in an unknown, lost tomb (Wellborn, p. 3).

2) During the Civil War the property was owned by the Parish of Orleans (ibid).

3) The previous owner was a philanthropist and misanthrope, John McDonough (a true oxymoron), who died in 1850, leaving no heirs (Ryan, p. 4).

4) There is no record of a Mona / Lisa ever having been associated with the property.

The legend and haunting have no historical validity; however, they are important in that this tale is a regional example of an endemic, urban myth. Virtually every American city has a story about a vengeful ghost venting her wrath upon passionate teenagers. These tales are part of the dark side of our Christian heritage. They are designed to defeat nature with the dagger of fear. Here we have a ghost given birth through neurotic guilt.

The Golden Children

Pierre Lefevre lived in a decrepit old double. It was on Saratoga Street and Jackson Avenue, facing the old cemetery.

Pierre designed his life to accomplish one task–the acquisition of gold. He worked several jobs. His free time, what little there was he squandered on making money. Year by year his cache of gold grew. When not pursuing gold or sleeping, he would sit in fascinated rapture gazing upon his . . . *beautiful little children* . . . (de Lavigne, p. 224).

Pierre sacrificed everything for his growing family. Friend was only a word. A lover or wife would hardly be cost effective. After all his children were his future. He rested assured that one day his children would allow him to live like a king. Until then he must love only them. Like all misers who have only one love, he had only one fear–Theft! Parsimonious Pierre constructed a safe in his chimney where his children would have care during the day while he worked. At night he assembled his issue on the decaying cot he called his bed. He would peer into their golden faces until Morpheus tore him from his ecstasy.

The years rolled into decades. Papa Pierre grew old. He knew that his children would never have the opportunity of caring for him in his retirement for now death would inherit that burden. Realizing this he knew he must provide for his progeny. The night of his death he gathered his gold and slid quietly into the night. Somewhere on his property he dug a new nest for his beloved. He dug it deep for he wanted his children to be safe and warm.

The next morning he danced with death. His neighbors and the authorities examined his home and property to find only the implimentia of a reclusive miser. No trace was ever found of his hoard.

Until his home was demolished in 1940 the residents of the area reported many instances of seeing the old man's shade roaming from the cemetery to his overgrown yard searching for his beautiful golden children (Ibid, p. 225). His treasure has never recovered.

Old Otto Krane

New Orleans, by and large, is below sea level. In order to preserve and extend dry land the early European colonists began to construct levees along the banks of the Mississippi and various bayous. The effort reached its zenith through the offices of Gen. P. G. T. Beauregard, who was a Creole gentleman, engineer, West Point graduate, distinguished in the Mexican War, Confederate General, founding member of the original Louisiana Lottery, prolific author and millionaire upon his death.

Levee is a French word which means a rising, embankment. A levee is usually constructed several meters away from the water's borders. The farther one moves away from a river, the higher is the ground (to a point). When a levee was constructed a phenomenon arose. The land between the river and the levee would sometimes be dry; sometimes flooded. That vanishing land is referred to as a batture. Batture is also French indicating an elevated portion of a river or sea bottom.

The batture creates a legal limbo. Since the land is not permanent no permanent rights can thereby be established. It is a *no man's* land where generations of people have constructed cabins, lean-tos, tents. These people live tax and rent free. Many of these bohemians plant sizeable gardens in the rich delta soil. The author while researching this story found a small community raising along with their gardens, goats, chickens, ducks and geese.

Typical Batture Cabin

Old Otto Krane is the story of one of the batture's residents. Circa 1878 a set of circumstances would waltz together that would create an enduring New Orleans ghost.

No one knew much about Old Otto except that he was ancient and had always seemed that way. Confederate veterans remembered the old boy long before the war and, of course, afterwards to 1878 (de Lavigne). He lived in a ramshackle old cabin that he built on an unused barge. He moored his cabin-barge to the levee so that during floods he would float, but be secure to his mooring. Otto lived a bare-boned existence. He collected and sold scrap; did odd jobs. Otto, like many before and after him, had a garden, fished, hunted and trapped. The aged recluse was also an accomplished herbalist making powders, potions and salves from the plentiful roots, herbs and barks that comprise the ecosystem of the batture. These he sold to faithful customers who exclaimed their virtues.

Old Otto had been a fixture on the batture for decades. People remarked that he appeared to be in his eighties before the Civil War and twenty plus years later he had not changed a hair. This unusual phenomenon was variously attributed to his acumen with herbs, Voo-Doo, witchcraft, the occult. When questioned about his longevity, Otto would cackle, *Ain't got nothin' to do wid nothin' but walkin'. I sometime walk a hunert miles in a week. Walkin' good for the blood. Good for the liva. Hell, man, good for evrythin'* (Ibid).

His prescription for his vigor and vitality was very strange since he hobbled along on two crude wooden legs given extra support by a thick, troubled, oak walking stick. When asked about his condition he would reply, *Cut me legs off meself when I was but five* (Ibid).

He was equally cryptic about his history. When he did answer personal questions his old voice would pour out sentences like, *Ain't from nowhere. Never know'd no fam'ly. Don' really think I knows nobody last name but mine–un* (Ibid).

Rumors abounded about Old Otto as they do about strange, reclusive people. It was reported that on occasion Otto would collect his mail at the post office. Among the few letters and an occasional parcel there would be a thick envelop with German stamps. Who was this strange man? Is it true that he hoarded gold? To where did he disappear on his sojourns, and how did he afford his travels?

The old man was indeed a curiosity. For the most part he simply went about his business in his eccentric way. He was close to only one person and that was the grandniece of Betty Barnes, the *great gossip*. Judy was nine years old and born of Irish stock. Her last name was McDowell. She had thick red hair and emerald green eyes. Her happy voice and quick mind impressed the old bachelor. He would sometimes sit with her for hours telling her stories, teaching her about herbs and legends, being her friend.

One day on the batture Old Otto's body was discovered at the beginning of Rousseau Street. He had been beaten viciously. His belly had been torn from chest to groin. His throat slashed. The primitive shack he called home had been ransacked. The authorities theorized that some thugs had accepted the rumors about a miser's treasure as fact.

When Judy heard of her friend's dreadful death her tears flowed like the river that revealed his body. She would many times sit by the river and remember Otto's kind eyes and fascinating stories. She mused about ghosts and wondered if maybe Old Otto was a ghost. If such is true where is her friend's ghost?

One dismal, storm-tortured night, Judy's mind obsessed on Otto's shade. He was alone in the storm. The shack he called home had been razed for firewood and building material. The thought of Otto's revenent homeless and battered in the stinging rain and slamming thunder pushed her fear invaded mind to the abyss. She rose from her bed and slipped into the vicious night wrapped in her threadbare blanket. The cold rain smashed into her skin like icy bullets. She ran toward Otto's cabin. Her brain burned with his presence. She could feel him; sense him. Before her on the spot hapless Otto's camp once stood she saw a magnificent light. As she approached it the warmth embraced her. The frigid fringes of the storm ended their pain.

Oh, Uncle Otto! she beamed. As her eyes search the light she saw a figure within. Her eyes struggled to make sense of the image. The emerging entity revealed itself as Otto Krane as he appeared in articulo morte (at the time of death). His thoughtful face had been broken and lacerated. Trembling hands held his organs and viscera vainly. Blood spurted through severed arteries. Despite the horror before her she felt no fear nor revulsion. Her old friend's love shone through the suffering ghost. Judy offered Otto her blanket. *You must be cold, Uncle Otto. Oh, Uncle Otto, I've missed you so much. Why did they have to kill you!? Why?! Why?!*

Otto reached out and wrapped the blanket around his mutilated body. He motioned Judy to follow him. She felt as though she were floating through the rain-soaked air. Their journey was magical. She experienced one of Otto's sojourns passing over bogs and bayous. Roads and villages and farmhouses greeted her senses with warmth and the aromas of friendship and love. Time vanished. The magnificence of her walk with Otto overwhelmed her.

Their journey ended on a mist shrouded road sheltered by magnificent cypress trees. Otto motioned silently for the girl to follow him. They walked slowly through the eternal beauty of the morning into the woods. A clearing appeared displaying a circle of ivory stones. The earth opened to reveal a black, iron strong box. Its heavy lid became transparent displaying a hoard of dazzling gold coins.   Otto muttered through his slashed throat—*Yours*.

The girl's next vision was the debatable comfort of her honest, raw home. She was manic. *Papa, Mama, Auntie, wake up, wake up, we have to go, please, please, we have to go. Come. Come. Otto's gold!*

The dazed household could not calm the girl's urgent pleading. Was the poor creature crazy? Had the night torn reason from her soul? Her cries were insistent.

They must go! After three days of madness her beleaguered family dragged together $2.85 to rent a horse and wagon for twenty-four hours. *Which way do we go*? her father inquired.

Why don't you see him? Follow Uncle Otto! Straight ahead . . . then a left on St. Charles, Judy stammered.

So went the entire ride. She knew the road. Remembered the hamlets and farms. Recalled the cypress and oak trees spreading their arms over the serpentine shell street. *Stop, stop, stop*, her screams echoed from the guardian trees. *Bring the shovel and ropes*" then she bolted from the cart and ran into the wilderness.

Her father followed her. She stopped. *Dig here*, *Papa*.

McDowell began what he thought was a futile exercise. His shovel pierced the bleeding earth without resistance. A gaping hole displayed only darkness. The smell of death reached his nostrils. *Why, what's this*? he questioned as he reached into the abyss to retrieve a blanket reeking of death.

It was the blanket Judy had given Otto that bleak night on the levee. *Why, Judy, this looks like your blanket? How . . ., why*?

His questions were soon stifled by the shining secret within the strong box shrouded by the blanket. With difficulty he and his family loaded their treasure and returned to New Orleans and a new life.

The literati believe love transcends death. Otto seconds their voice.

The Shell Road Spectre

During the sweaty month of September, in the year of our Lord 1852, word spread like the pox through the bawdy houses and among the crib whores lining the upper portion of Bienville Street. At that time the twenty-eight hundred block and running was defined by a shell road. In the Gulf South such thoroughfares are common. For centuries the exoskeletons of oysters, clams and their kin were used to create very serviceable roads. As hoof and foot trooped these lanes they shattered and compacted to form relatively smooth, stable highways. Rain, manure, urine combined for further solidification. At night during a full moon they glisten and shine like the strands of a silent spider's web.

Bienville Street was then populated by little shacks called cribs. Within these structures cheap whores provided cheaper thrills. Tiny Toots, Big Annie or French Lou (de Lavigne, p. 40) would *willingly befriend* gentlemen for a seated liberty quarter.

Pimps and hustlers offered girls, opium, absinthe, gin, whiskey for dimes. Sailors and ruffians sometime scuffled in the miasmic mist. Free Negroes prowled the environs looking for discarded bottles, lost change or sleeping drunks. Muggers cracked skulls and emptied pockets. Such was the neighborhood Adam Quigley called home. Quigley had traveled mightily. He was born in Connecticut of Yankee Protestant stock. Before coming to New Orleans he had been among the hoard who descended upon California in '49. Two years later he and his burro Nellie surfaced in New Orleans. He had relatives in the Crescent City.

Young Mentor Quigley was his grandnephew. They met by happenstance.   Mentor was a druggist who was forever experimenting with extracts and flavorings. One day, lost in his thoughts about his formulae, he was beset by highwaymen. The unfortunate chemist was beaten and robbed. Adam stumbled upon him and provided aid. In the course of their conversation, the men discovered their kinship. Soon old Adam became a frequent guest of Mentor's family. When Adam departed he would always leave a freshly minted gold eagle.

The old man loved Mentor and his wife and their children. One night he confided to his nephew that he had struck it rich in the gold fields. He had a treasure that one day would belong to the druggist.

Listen, if you have ears to hear, the mocking bird in the cypress tree watched me bury it. But, all she saw was me back. Not them old black shit eatin' beetles though. No siree, they saw me face to face. Looked right at me they did! Didn't care none. Kept right on dining on dung, Ha, Ha, Ha, hee, hee, hee.

Shortly after that episode around dawn two John's stumbled upon the corpse of an old man. His throat had been slashed brutally. What had once been a face dominated by twinkling blue eyes was a gore encrusted mask dressed with green, iridescent flies.

The men hurried to report the felony. When they returned with police the corpse was gone. Shortly after this incident the ghastly ghost began his haunt. Reports flooded the precinct. Men armed with pistols and clubs and holy water hunted and kept vigil. The reports increased. Terror reigned.

Mentor learned of his great uncle's death through the newspaper. He initiated his own investigation. He learned nothing the newspaper had not revealed. Mentor repaired to the old man's cabin located scant yards from where his remains had been discovered, then lost. Behind the shack lay the festering remains of his companion Nellie. A second victim of that infamous eve of destruction. The shed that was Adam's home had been ransacked. His few possessions were scattered and shattered. Floor boards had been ruptured. The mattress slashed. Holes cratered his vegetable garden. Chicks roamed aimlessly. No gold. No treasure.

A mockingbird's cry excited the evening. Adam's words tolled across Mentor's mind. He ran into the waning light. Back turned to the bird's voice he surveyed the scene. Before his eyes he noticed lumps ascending from the edge of the serpentine shell trail. Stealthily his feet pulled him forward. His eyes fixed on the mounds.

Délie, Délie, he beckoned to his wife, *come and see. Mon Cheri, what is it? What have you found.*

Look here, Mon Aimée, these two disturbances, the first one displays a line of black beetles feasting on feces! Don't you remember what Uncle Adam said about the bird to his back and the beetles before his eyes?

Before she could answer a coach thundered toward them. They hid in the tall weeds. The carriage held three loud pimps and their painted harlots. The horses bolted. A pale revenent, throat a tattered fissure, thundered an unearthly wail. Strumpets screamed. Pimps fired pistols. Panic exploded. Pandemonium extended her spectre.

Mentor and Délie watched in silence as the whirling ghost drove the miscreants away. The apparition remained. It was Uncle Adam! The fear he generated was replaced by the warmth of love. He floated above the first, smaller hill of stones smiling and pointing down. The mesmerized couple began to dig. After a dozen spades iron rang out. The more they dug the better they could see the strong box. It was heavy, black iron with rivets securing its sides. The loose shells and moist soil relinquished their grasp. Inside the sturdy safe were row upon row of 1850-S double eagles. A fortune. Also therein was a notarized will which had been witnessed by six load men. Mentor recognized three of the names as those who were visited by Adam's ghost just moments before on the shell road. As he discussed this and their fortune with his wife Adam's shade reappeared. The mutilated ghost pointed to the larger, as yet undisturbed mound.

Dig! Rumbled through his gashed throat.

Within moments the couple were facing a festering corpse.

It was Adam's remains. They quickly reported their discoveries to Officer Bolonsa. The police were a bit recalcitrant about reopening the case. After all, they had beat a confession out of the municipal moron and would soon be hanging the wretch.   Notwithstanding, justice was served.   The true murderers were hanged. Mentor and Délie used their fortune well. And Old Adam Quigley rested forevermore under a marble headstone that joined him and his family in the eternity of the rich, ripe soil of Louisiana.

The Old Spanish Garrison

For generations the folk of New Orleans have spoken in dread whispers about the pantheon of mutilated ghosts that prowl this elegant structure with broken fingers holding butchered genitalia, gaping eye sockets set ablaze with burning pitch. And, the most dreadful of all, many witnesses swore to having seen half-a-dozen or more nude men–their silent mouths gaping holes of pain. Bound around their sweat-stained, bare waists were iron kettles. The bottom of the kettles had been heated to a dull red forcing the two or three spectral rats inside to gnaw their way through the guts of their restrained hosts.

This story had gained such status that it was represented in several bibliographies. Upon researching the site, the author ascertained that the building was not erected until 1834–thirty-one years after the Spanish evacuated the city. It was included because it is a classic example of a species of folklore, and as such was deemed to be of anthropological significance.

Shortly after *New Orleans Ghosts* went to press, the author discovered facts which do indeed substantiate this site as actually haunted. Built in 1834, the edifice could not possibly have been in existence during the Spanish occupation. This fact was noted by the author. It seemed as though the author disproved an old ghost story; however, it was included because of its value as folklore. Nevertheless, one day the author met a gentlemen who lived in the building. I related the story to him about the erroneous haunting. He then told me that he had experienced a variety of very strange happenings, all of which had the earmarks of a classical ghost story. He alleged that cold spots, noises and ghastly odors occurred without all of which were without rational explanation. This information compelled me to do further research on the site.

On 25 April 1862, Admiral Farragut defeated the Confederate forces assigned to defend the city and docked at the port with fourteen warships, a dozen mortar boats, and five thousand Marines and Sailors. Henry Bell went ashore with the full complement of Marines and two brass howitzers. Captain Theodorus Bailey and Lieutenant George H. Perkins demanded the surrender of the city, its garrison and commander General Mansfield Lovell. Mayor John T. Monroe refused to surrender, thus forcing an armed takeover and occupation. Monroe's actions provided time for Confederate General Lovell and the majority of his forces to retreat from the city they failed to defend. This resistance engineered ill feelings between victor and vanquished that sustained itself until federal troops were finally withdrawn from the city in 1877 under the administration of Rutherford B. Hayes.

The city was ruled by a succession of military governors, the first of whom was Benjamin Franklin Butler. It was under Butler's administration that the property in question was converted to a union jail in order to house confederates too unlucky, sick, demoralized, drunk or stupid to escape with Lovell. Conditions in the prison were deplorable. Disease was rampant. Brutality was the norm. Malnutrition, the bill of fare. Latrines were overflowing buckets.

The jail also held recalcitrant officials and citizens and the final outrage–a certain number of the city's genteel ladies. Butler did a fairly good job. He was a brilliant administrator. He restored civil order, disciplined his troops, repaired levees and docks, improved sanitation and levied taxes. Butler ordered his officers and men to show courtesy and respect to the people of the defeated city. The courtesy was not returned. The ladies of the gentry seemed to make a concerted effort to insult and demean Butler's troops. Not one to turn the other cheek, the general issued the following order:

General Order *Headquarters Department of the Gulf*
No. 28   New Orleans, May 15, 1802.

As the officers and soldiers of the United States have been subject to repeated insults from the women [calling themselves ladies] of New Orleans, in return for the most scrupulous non-interference and courtesy on our part, it is ordered that hereafter when any female shall by word, gesture, or movement, insult or show contempt for any officer or soldier of the United States, she shall be regarded and held liable to be treated as a woman of the town plying her avocation.

By command of MAJOR-GENERAL BUTLER and GEOR. C. STRONG, A.A. Gen., Chief of Staff.

Several women were soon arrested and ensconced in the filthy confines of the military prison. Imprisonment, disease, torture, brutality, death were difficult enough for soldiers to face, but civilian women who were the flowers of the city's establishment were an affront worthy of only Satan. The misery and death and insults burned into Creole and Southern sensibilities. The brutality of the unwanted Spanish under Alejandro O'Reilly and the brutishness of the conquering Yankees merged into one legend. Time distorted facts. History blurred. Fact and fiction merged into one.

La Pharmacie Française

Pharmacies have their origin in pre-history. Shamans, Wiccans, priestesses began the practice of dispensing herbs, potions, powders, elixirs. As civilizations developed, so did pharmacology. The pharmacies of the New World contributed as much to civilization and science as did their Old World progenitors. Coca Cola, Moxie, 7-Up, thousands of medicines and compounds, as well as a tremendous corpus of research were generated by American pharmacies.

La Pharmacie Française

The first licensed pharmacy in the United States was opened for business in New Orleans in 1823. Louis J. Dufilho, Jr. specifically built his apothecary shop on rue Chartres to accommodate his unique document. His shop prospered to the point that he counted among his property twenty-three slaves. Like apothecaries throughout time, he combined his knowledge with indigenous remedies and observations. European, Creole, African and Native American pharmacopeia merged in the pregnant atmosphere of the Crescent City to create bitters, hot sauces, and even the original *cocktail*. In the late 18th century a New Orleans pharmacist Antoine Peychaud dispensed tonics mixed with various liquors and his invention, Peychaud Bitters. He served his libations in egg cups (French-coquetier). The American influence or maybe the drink itself corrupted the word into *cocktail* (see Appendix B).

African influences in Louisiana's emerging culture were stronger here than in other parts of the United States because of our French origins. The French instituted the *Code Noir* which was a codification of the rights and privileges of "people of color" whether free or slave. These Black Codes allowed blacks greater chances to integrate and merge with the dominant European culture. Voo-Doo, Creole cooking, art, jazz, rag-time, legends and rituals found fertile soil in which to flourish under such a system.

La Pharmacie Française influenced by the sub-culture of Marie Laveau, Dr. John and nameless others displays a large stock Voo-Doo-inspired remedies. Traditions carry the message that Monsieur Dufilho's shop dispensed more than Voo-Doo inspired aids. Among Voo-Doo practitioners, local and alien, the shop is a must-do for rituals. Dr. Dufilho was a scientist and as such a curious man. There can be no doubt that he adopted and adapted more than one elixir from his chattel. He was also Creole as defined as a person of French and/or Spanish origin born in North America. Creole can also be defined as a person who can trace her antebellum heritage to a French and/or Spanish (European) father usually and an African/African-American mother. Such a class was usually birthed by the quaint practice of quadroon balls. At these galas aristocratic Caucasians, male Creoles, were introduced to mixed-rare females. Essentially, these liaisons resulted in two families for the bon-vivants. Each had its integrity, privileges, restrictions. In such a liberal environment, Voo-Doo gathered over time almost as much significance for the white master as it did for the black slave.

The notion of this building's being haunted is silent in the bibliographic record, however, it is seconded by many French Quarter residents. On that basis an interview was conducted.

No staff member reported any paranormal activity. In fact, several were surprised by my inquiries. As can be seen in the Appendix the museum speaks of Voo-Doo and potions, but makes no mention of ghosts nor hauntings.

SO MOTE IT BE!

The Ghost and the Chessboard

On Saint John's Eve (24 June originally a traditional Celtic fire festivals) Marie Laveau's legions of spectral followers have been rumored to return for a ritual of lust and concupiscence. Drums sound primordial rhythms to which the naked revelers embrace and fall into ecstatic pleasures. Ectoplasmic serpents entwine themselves among legs and hips, throats and genitals. The air is pregnant with perverse passions. The liturgy climaxes with the manifestation of Obi, the Great Serpent Benefactor.

Midnight vaporizes the scene leaving only miasmic mist and, some say, a pale figure lost is thought over a solitary game of chess. A name belongs to the ghostly chess player. He lies buried a few meters from Marie. He is Paul Charles Morphy.

If Morphy was not remembered for his hauntings he would still hold history's attention. Morphy was born 22 June 1837 the son of a powerful aristocratic New Orleans family. He benefitted from a superb education and was fluent in a half of a dozen languages. His true genius lay in his mastery of Chess. Alonzo Morphy, his father, taught him the fundamentals of the game at age ten. By twelve he defeated such chess nobles as General Winfield Scott and Grand Masters J. D. Lowenthal and Eugene Rousseau. In 1857 his stunning victories at the American Chess Congress in New York confirmed him as America's premier chess wizard. He traveled Europe until 1840 defeating all comers. Morphy was hailed as a world champion. Success only brought increasing cynicism from the eccentric savant. The politics and finances of the professional aspect of the game embittered him. He returned to New Orleans where he became increasingly disturbed.   The champion became a recluse. Although passionately heterosexual he indulged in transvestism. His other great interest during his dark decline was gorging himself on his favorite food—shrimp.

During his self-imposed New Orleans exile he lived at several addresses at which he also left his imprint. The Beauregard-Keyes House mentioned in *New Orleans Ghosts* as a ghost dormitory also boasts a record of his silent games as well as Brennan's Restaurant, Royal Street.

Acme Oyster House

On many occasions this author has enjoyed succulent seafood and ice cold beer at the Acme Oyster House. After becoming known as a writer of ghost stories, several staff, as well as customers, regaled me with tales about the curious phenomena held within the aged walls.   What I heard impressed me to the extent that I knew the stories would be represented in any sequel I elected to write in the future. The future arrived and 3 March 1999 marked my arrival at Acme Oyster House to begin my research on an amazing set of data.

My primary contact was Glen Armantrout.   He presents himself as an intelligent, pragmatic business person. I sought him out. He has no agenda in sharing information with this author. The restaurant he manages does a thriving business based on good food and service.   I have no problem approaching Mr. Armantrout as an objective witness within this criteria.

I learned that the structure replaced a previous one destroyed in the great fire of 1795. It was used as a home and office by Louis Lioteau. This Creole gentleman was a man of means, who, judging by the slave quarters, owned over a dozen slaves. The property is first mentioned 9 November 1814 in the Testament de Louis Lioteau who bequeathed it to his wife Lucile Vivant 4 November 1831. From 1831 to 1924 the history of the building is unremarkable. Or, at least, Mr. Armantrout had no knowledge to the contrary. 24 February 1924 changed all of that. A fire ravaged the block destroying the portion of the edifice which stood at 117-119 Royal Street. The conflagration also claimed the life of veteran firefighter Captain Jules Pujol. A large portion of M. Lioteau's original buildings were destroyed. What remained is now the Acme Oyster House. Saloons, restaurants and oyster houses have been the main economy of the property since the mid-nineteenth century and the property's acquisition by one Shepherd Brooks in 1871. As such, no doubts, there were fights, robberies, death. Nevertheless, I have found no bibliographic record of any paranormal activity. When I first heard of these stories, I tended to dismiss them as so much barroom bull shit–that is, until I finished my interviews and concluded my research.

Mr. Armantrout, after providing a brief history of his plant, related his paranormal experiences. *We always had electrical problems. TV's would turn on for no reason. Lights flickered. Sometimes electrical equipment downstairs would just go out. At first, I excused it as a result of old wiring, circuitry, that sort of thing. After a while I noticed that it always occurred around dusk. Not everyday, but when it did happen it was always around sunset. (It should be mentioned that the majority of ghostly sightings, worldwide, happen during the hours of dawn and dusk.) About two years ago we renovated the place. Part of that renovation included rewiring, circuit breakers and a state of the art security system. No sooner was the equipment installed than it started firing off. The security company re-calibrated the equipment to lessen its sensitivity. No luck. We had to abandon the high tech stuff for an older, electrical not electronic system. We still had problems, but not as bad.*

These anomalies were of such consistent mystery that the management, in their desperation, was open-minded enough to enlist the aid of paranormal investigators. The chief investigator, Larry Montz, is a trained electrical engineer who has done some outstanding paranormal research. He has a reputation for honesty and integrity.

After several days, the scientists discovered a variety of electromagnetic and thermal aberrations. They concluded that the activity was strongest on the third floor. This conclusion was seconded by several employees, as well as Mr. Armantrout, who reported *eerie feelings* whenever they ventured there.   Mr. Montz's research was so compelling that several television programs are interested in further investigations.

I next interviewed Michael Broadway, *head shucker*, an eighteen year employee of the establishment. Anyone who has ever had the pleasure of eating raw oysters has met that breed of homo sapiens known as the *oyster shucker*. Beside having a facility for opening the delicious bivalves, these guys will entertain their guests with stories about oysters and oyster eaters that will fascinate, beguile, bemuse and bewitch their listeners. It was from these stories, some would say tall tales, that the phrase *shuck and jive* originated.   Among the sub-culture of oyster shuckers names like Dr. O., The Elder, Cherokee Charlie and Big Daddy Fats are the material of legend.   Mr. Broadway of Acme is a man who respects and nurtures that tradition.   After all his teacher and predecessor was Dr. O.

The first thing he mentioned during our interview was his observation about the peculiar environment manifest on the third floor.   Rat traps were tripped, but no rat.   Furniture was moved with no one's taking the credit.   Footfalls announced unseen sources. Most of the employees avoid that area. [Mr. Broadway also said that an old cook, an octogenarian, by the name of Mr. Nick, told him that during the twenties and thirties, the Acme was frequented by gamblers like Diamond Jim Moran and various black-hand henchmen. Seemingly, the third floor hosted gambling and private parties.] Evidently, the Acme has a more colorful history than I originally thought.

Enough said. It was now incumbent upon me to climb the stairs and investigate this notorious floor for myself.   I was accompanied by the manager, Mr. Armantrout. Upon ascending the stairs, the first thing that drew my attention was the severe angle of the staircase.   It listed a full 30° out of square.   The third floor was hot, close, uncomfortable, dusty. After all I heard I was confronted with a plain, common, dirty attic. As we moved farther to the rear of the room we came face-to-face with a chilling mystery.   I recorded our experience on 35mm film; several exposures are displayed on these pages.

Halfway to the rear of the attic was a bleached pigeon's skeleton. Further examination revealed that the bony structure was intact perfectly. As evidenced by the photographs, the bones appeared as if they were prepared for a museum. Had the Aves death been the product of some predator the remains would have been scattered helter-skelter. They were not.

Pidgeon Victim

The remains were not mummified. There is virtually no trace of dried tissue clinging to the carcass. We smelled no decay, no putrescence. Given the environmental conditions of the top floor (humid/hot/dimly lit), the condition described is impossible without some outside agency. What became of the flesh? Why is there no evidence of blood or other bodily fluids? How were they removed, and who or what disposed of them?

A final consideration deepens the mystery. The feathers are approximately one meter from the corpse. Their position indicates that they were removed methodically. The condition of the feathers revealed that they could not be too old for only a hint of dust covered their surfaces. Also, the symmetrical pattern of plumage indicated a recent origin. They had been only slightly disturbed by draughts and vermin. Had their tenure

Feather Felony

been greater, their dispersal pattern would have been more chaotic.

Glenn seemed as amazed and perplexed as I. After exposing about a dozen frames, I asked him a few questions. *When was the last time he was up there?*
About a month ago.
Had anything like that happened before?
No!
Do you have any explanation for this weirdness?
No!
My questioning netted me virtually no information to explain the bizarre conditions we witnessed and I photographed. Reflecting on the experience, I equated it with a similar situation to which I was privy. It is documented in my first book, *New Orleans Ghosts*. While researching a story titled, *A Haunted House*, the individual I interviewed showed me a room that had been occupied by a sea captain who smuggled slaves and

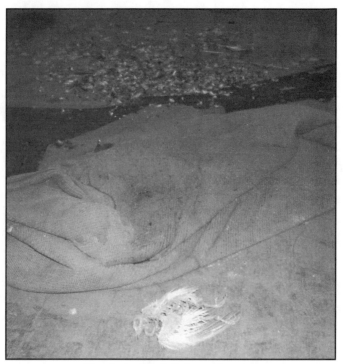

Undisturbed Crime Scene

practiced Voo-Doo. In this particular case, the shade of the old captain was malevolent, evil. His arcane powers seemed to exist past his death. I wonder about any similarities Acme might share with the *Haunted House*?

What I do know is that the Acme Oyster House is ripe for an in depth scientific examination. Perhaps this story will encourage a serious investigation by competent researchers.

Lafitte's Blacksmith Shop

Fire ripped her blazing talons into the belly of the city on two momentous occasions during her colorful colonial period, Good Friday, 1788, and again on the Feast of the Immaculate Conception, 1794. Up until the last fire New Orleans was a city constructed of wooden buildings huddled together on the banks of the Mississippi. Essentially, it was a fire trap as history disastrously proclaimed on two horrific occasions. Both fires claimed over one thousand buildings and hundreds of lives. Spurred by these disasters, the Spanish Colonial government issued building ordinances which forbade wooden roofs, mandated fire walls between buildings, encouraged the use of fireproof building materials, controlled the accumulation of trash, and established fire responses.

One of the first buildings to conform to these new regulations and one of the earliest existing buildings in the French Quarter was the structure that came to be known as Lafitte's Blacksmith Shop. It exhibits a construction method called *briqueté entre poteaux* (bricked between posts).

Jean Lafitte (C1780-C1826) was a man of mystery. There are no verified records of his early life. He and his brother Pierre and an equally mysterious figure, Dominique You, first come to light around 1806. This trio collected a band of cutthroats and under a *lettre de marque* commissioned by the government of Cartagena (a short-lived Latin American dictatorship) began a relentless attack as privateers on everything afloat. He and his buccaneers headquartered in

Barataria Bay, south of New Orleans. It has become legend that the little shop on rue Bourbon was the conduit through which his plunder found its way to the merchants of New Orleans. Slaves, liquor, spices, textiles, weapons, all allegedly vomited from this modest structure to enrich tradesmen and pirates alike whose greatest commonality was Gold!

The War of 1812 again witnessed the fledgling United States

One of the oldest structures in the Vieux Carre

raped by the pugnacious English bulldog. Washington, D.C. was burned. American sailors were impressed and tortured. Soldiers died. Civilians were murdered. Women raped. The blood-stained tentacles of the insatiable British Empire probed the soft underbelly of our young republic. A force of 10,000 seasoned British troups under the Duke of Wellington's brother-in-law, General Sir Edward Packingham, prepared to capture New Orleans.

For reasons known only to himself, Jean Lafitte elected to ally himself with Andrew Jackson. The battle was a resounding victory for the Americans. Lafitte became a hero. President James Madison pardoned him. Around 1826, the fierce pirate completely disappeared from history.

Before my first book *New Orleans Ghosts* appeared, I cannot recall the existence of any *ghost tours* in the French Quarter.

Since the appearance of my work, it seems as though the only tours available in the Quarter are occult (ghost, vampire, werewolf, phantom) tours. While researching this work *New Orleans Ghost II*, I went on two different tours. Both of these tours concluded at the Blacksmith Shop where the participants could relax, talk about spookie things and enjoy reasonably priced, generous cocktails. It was during these interludes that I became aware of the fact that a substantial number of people who experienced the tours had taken pictures of the various sites as well as photographs inside the old shop only to find that many of these last snapshots exhibited strange, luminous, somewhat amorphous, translucent cloudlike images.   I examined several photos in the possession of some participants given them by friends and relations on previous tours. They were amazing in their number and consistency. I made approximately one dozen exposures on three separate occasions to no avail.

I interviewed both tour guides who informed me that participants showing up with photos of this nature was a relatively common occurrence. The bartenders also reported the existence of cold spots (a common *ghostly* phenomenon), electrical anomalies, and sounds without cause or distinct origin.

I found the bibliographic record mute regarding this most obvious haunting. Time limited my ability to conduct any in-depth analysis of the site that would net me hard data (photos, recording, etc.).   Nevertheless, from my experience with interviews, I have concluded that this site is very probably haunted. It is my recommendation that when you're in New Orleans and after you've read my books and looked for specters and shades you retire to Lafitte's Blacksmith Shop, knock down a few cocktails, take some photos and see what happens. If your photos reveal unexplained lights or shapes or entities, I request that you forward them to this author for inclusion in my subsequent works. Stick with me, baby, and I'll make ya famous!

Victor C. Klein
P. O. Box 9028
Metairie, LA 70005-9028   USA

Pontalba Buildings

These famous structures have a carefully documented and well-known history. Bienville cleared land and began the construction of New Orleans 16 April 1718. Le Blond de la Tour and his assistant, Adrien de Pauger, surveyed the land and drew the plans for New Orleans. What evolved can be seen today as what the locals call Jackson Square. St. Louis Cathedral, flanked by the Cabildo and the Presbytere circa 1796, face the river through a public square Place d'Armes, renamed Jackson Square in 1851. Running parallel to the square are the Pontalba Buildings completed also in 1851. It is arguably the most *beautiful town square in the USA*. The land bordering the *Square* served a multitude of purposes through an equal number of structures. Fires, hurricanes and rebuildings kept any edifices in a state of flux until the Baroness Pontalba arrived (1795-1874).

The Baroness, born Micaela Almonester, was a unique power in the Crescent City. Her history began in 1795 as the first daughter of Don Andrès Almonester Roxas q.v., aged 70, and his wife Louise de la Ronde aged 29. Two years after her birth sister Andrea arrived only to depart this life four years later. At six years of age she was heir and only child of a 71-year-old real estate tycoon and financial genius. Her father died at age 79. Her youthful mother soon remarried. Her new husband was the French Consul at New Orleans, Jean Baptiste Castillon. Five years later he died leaving widow and orphan among the richest citizens in the state of Louisiana. Her life was not happy. She was educated by the strict Ursulines Nuns. She dressed as a child and played with dolls until her arranged marriage with her cousin, Joseph Xavier Celestin Delfau de Pontalba of Mont L'Eveque, France. Her first meeting with him was the day of their marriage in Europe.

Micaela had fiery red hair and a temper to match. Celestin, or Tin-Tin as he was affectionately known, was a beautiful, emasculated fop. Micaela received a title from Tin-Tin and three sons: Celestin, Alfred and Gaston, and very little else. They lead separate lives. She in Paris where she indulged her passions for whatever various amusements that city had to offer. He, with his indomitable father, the Baron, at their country estate Chateau Mont L'Eveque. That their marriage was strained was attested to by Celestin's having "left" his young wife twice. Also, the old Baron disliked Micaela's willfulness in all matters, especially financial. Disgusted with her life in France, she returned to her great wealth in New Orleans with the title, Baroness Pontalba, and immediately filed for divorce. Such an act, suing for divorce, by a woman, no less, caused a minor scandal.

While in New Orleans she managed the great wealth she inherited from her father and step-father. New Orleans was going through its *golden age* fueled by the labor of slaves, the cotton gins and the steam boat. The Baroness wholeheartedly engaged in the city's commerce and social life.

In 1834, she returned to France in order to find an equitable solution to her and Celestin's marriage problem. Her family dilemma expanded to include her oldest son, Celestin, Jr., who deserted military school to live with her in Paris. This exacerbated her relations with her father-in-law, who excised his grandson from his will. A potentially scandalous divorce, a shattered family's taking sides: the hatred of an in-law all contributed to the Baroness' feelings of frustration and despair. Little was she aware of the future danger that awaited her.

The old Baron hated Micaela. Brooding in his dark chateau, he hatched the ultimate plan. He invited her to Mont l'Eveque ostensibly to attempt a reconciliation. 18 October 1834 she arrived.   Immediately she was ensconced in a "little chateau reserved for the use of visitors" (Garvey et al., 106).

Her father-in-law kept vigil on the smaller chateau.   As evening faded into night he saw the servants depart.   He had waited for this moment as the four loaded and primed, heavy caliber dueling pistols attested.   Dark shadows pursued him as he hobbled over the lawn and toward his Honor.   Bursting into the house, he climbed the stairs to his daughter-in-law's room. The confrontation was vitriolic; savage.   Shots exploded the still, black air.   The heavy lead balls found their marks.   One of them tore two fingers from her left hand.   Three more slammed into her heaving chest.   With the fury of Rasputin, she slammed the old felon onto the floor and tore from the smoke-filled room.   At the head of the steps her strength disappeared.   She tumbled down the polished, marble stairs.   Regaining his consciousness, the old malefic resumed his quest.   His eyes found her crumpled, blood-soaked form where her fall had left her. Satisfied that justice had been served, Monsieur Le Baron retired to Micaela's bedroom.   Loaded two pistols.   Placed both barrels against his thundering heart and pulled the triggers (Garvey, p. 106; Leavitt, p. 102).

The next morning the servants found last night's artifacts. Incredibly, our dear Micaela survived!   The scandal rocked the French-speaking world.   Our heroine's adventure netted her some grisly scars, and a huge fortune by way of marriage and inheritance.

After an extended stay in Europe, she returned to New Orleans at the age of fifty-three to begin the grandest of her plans, and the one by which we know her today. She recognized that the land that would soon hold her buildings was not enjoying optimum use.   Fortunately, for her and history, the property was also part of her vast holdings.

She envisioned a parallel set of 16 row houses. The bottom floor would be occupied by stores (as they still are today) with the second and third floors and attics occupied by the business owners and their families. It must be remarked that contrary to popular knowledge, the Pontalba Buildings were not intended as apartment houses, and, therefore, hold no claim to being the "oldest apartment houses in America" (Cowan et al., p. 226).

Micaela saw the venture as a way to organize and stimulate commerce. Her venture also added a pleasing symmetry to the city she so passionately loved.

The buildings are elegant; sublime. Her structures were her own design. They display no particular reference to any period. They are four-story edifices constructed of red brick with sumptuous balconies bordered by ornate iron grill work (a hallmark of the French Quarter) designed by Waldemar Talen (Garvey, p. 106; Leavitt, p. 102) The iron work displays the monogram AP (Almonester-Pontalba).

The Baroness proved to be a very difficult task master. She originally engaged the renowned architect James Gallier (Gallier Hall) as her builder. They argued constantly over cost, design, time tables, etc., etc., etc. She replaced him with Henry Howard, another architect with a glowing reputation (Howard Avenue). They also had their share of quarrels. Synthesizing the plans and specifications of Gallier and Howard, she finally found them completed by Samuel–long suffering–Stewart.

The Upper Pontalba (St. Peter Street) was finished in 1850. The Lower Pontalba (St. Ann Street) was completed February 1851. Total cost for the buildings was $300,000. In 1982, the City of New Orleans spent $10 million on their renovation and preservation (Leavitt, p. 102). They are a national historic landmark.

Baroness Pontalba and her sons occupied suites in the Upper Pontalba. From her porch she then began the renovation of the Place d'Armes. Madame commissioned Clark Mills to create a magnificent equestrian statue of Andrew Jackson, hero of the Battle of New Orleans (15 January 1815). She petitioned and was granted permission to rename the Place d'Armes *Jackson Square*. She also paid for the magnificent iron fence that, to this day, still surrounds the impressive square.

Given the colorful history of the Baroness Pontalba what with intrigues, hints of sexual improprieties, desertions, violence, murder and scandal it came as a great surprise to the author to discover that the ghost that haunts the Upper Pontalba Building has nothing to do with its famous creator. Instead, the ghost that dances and sings in the beautiful, red edifice is none other than the Swedish nightingale Jenny Lind (1820-87). The best and most succinct account of this unlikely haunting can be found in *The Times-Picayune* account which is here reprinted in its entirety.

Ghosts Preserve the Golden Era

In the center residence of the Upper Pontalba Building, formerly the famed Jenny Lind residence, is noted for ballroom dancing and music from around the 1850s (the Golden Era of New Orleans was 1830-1860).

Jenny Lind arrived in New Orleans Feb. 6, 1851, sponsored by P.T. Barnum and gave 12 concerts at the St. Charles Theater. She was honored at her residence with a parade. She donated money to the firemen for their uniforms. She stayed in the finest residence of all in the Pontalbas.

Usually, on a full moon in February, the large center ballroom and front parlor is crowded with ectoplasm (fog), music and laughter. A happy occasion perhaps! No unresolved events. One can feel the happiness!

Mayor T. Semmes Walmsley's wife occupied the residence in the 1940s and reported occurrences of the dancing and joyous times, along with a prominent judge who lived in the rowhouse before Mrs. Walmsley.

Current resident Thomas Cook allowed the British Broadcasting Corporation to film the famous ballroom ghosts recently and it was shown on Lifetime Television in conjunction with an Anne Rice special in October 1994.

Every haunting investigated to date by this author has revealed that the alleged ghost, shade, revenent had some intimate connection to the site. The person in question lived, loved and/or died on the possessed premises. This case is the exception to what I previously thought was a *law* concerning hauntings.

Cabildo

The detested Spanish governor of Louisiana, Don Alejandro O'Reilly, designed and built the present day Cabildo in 1795, using several hundred slaves to complete the bloody task. The Illustrious Cabildo, as it was called, was the administrative center of the Louisiana colony and housed the various political mechanisms established in 1769 when Spain assumed control of the territory from France according to the secret Treaty of Fountainbleau. As such, the Cabildo was the site of much blood letting. Slaves were sold in its shadow. Executioning by firing squad, garrote and gallows were the preferred remedy for scores of crimes that today would be punished by fines, if at all.

The most heinous of the executions performed by permission of the Illustrious Cabildo took place on its grounds in 1769. Here six French colonial (Creole) aristocrats found death at the hands of Spanish justice. France ceded the Louisiana Territory to Spain by way of the Treaty of Fountainbleu 1768. When news of this reached New Orleans, the citizenry was appalled. They petitioned Louis XV to take them back into the security of the French Empire. In their desperation their appeals even sounded in the ears of England's George II. Anything would be preferable to the dreaded idea of Spanish hegemony (Leavitt).

Finally, 5 March 1766 Don Antonio de Ulloa arrived as the first Spanish governor (see *New Orleans Ghosts*, pp. 51-57). He was indecisive. Inept. His two greatest blunders were trying to control the illegal aspects of the slave trade, and limiting the alcoholic beverages of the colony to only Spanish products. Nooses were tied. Muskets and pistols primed and powdered. Sabers, rapiers, dirks were sharpened and buffed.

Then, the final and most horrific insult. Ulloa, a 50-year-old scientist and scholar, married a 19-year-old dark-skinned Indian Princess from Beleise. The women of the city were outraged. The fire of rebellion ignited and drove Ulloa and his *mestiso whore* from the city.

From 1 November 1768 until 16 August 1769, New Orleans and for that matter the entire Louisiana territory was ruled by anarchy. On that August day Spain resumed control with the iron fist of Don Alejandro O'Reilly. Arriving with 24 ships, 2,000 marines and 50 cannon and his good friend and cohort, Don Aldrès Almonster Roxas *q.v.*, the father of the future Baroness Pontalba q.v., O'Reilly quickly regained control of the city. He arrested twelve leaders of the revolt and executed five; a sixth died from bayonet wounds. He left the shattered bodies to rot in the radiant August sunshine. (For a more detailed history of this see *New Orleans Ghosts*, pp. 51-54).

Only a few years before this episode of Spanish justice, French justice played out on these same blood-soaked grounds. A crime wave ravaged the city. A chicken was stolen. Almost as suddenly a pig was reported missing. Then clothes on a clothes line disappeared. The French authorities threw their full weight and resources into the investigation. Thanks to a lucky tip by a responsible and vigilant citizen, the powers that be learned that a large, Negro slave by the name of Ceasar had been observed gorging himself sumptiously and clandestinely on pork chops and fried chicken all the while dressed in the clothes of a gentleman. His arrest and trial were over in hours.

His punishment:

1) Stripped naked and whipped on back and buttocks until black ribbons of flesh revealed oozing, red muscle.

2) Burned on the cheek with the mark of a thief.

3) Tendons of both hands severed leaving only useless claws.

4) Broken on the wheel (Leavitt, p. 42).

5) Body thrown in river.

Such acts of brutality are alleged to leave a *psychic imprint* on the environment in which they happen (Klein, p. 107ff). If this is true, then the present day Cabildo rests on fertile ground. I have found some bibliographic reference to the alleged hauntings of the Cabildo; however, ghost lore has become the stock and trade of French Quarter tour guides since the publication of *New Orleans Ghosts*. Part of their litany about the Cabildo hauntings was related to this author by a tour guide (let us call her Denise Schear). The following is her tale.

During the new moon in December, the darkest month of the year, it has been whispered for generations that Marie Laveau bequeathed a dark legacy to the Crescent City. Although a Voo-Doo priestess, she was also a devout Roman Catholic. Such a situation is indeed quite common. Voo-Doo like Christianity is a synergetic religion. Both owe their identities to bits and pieces borrowed, appropriated, stolen from other faiths. Marie obtained the holy water, candles, incense she used in her occult rituals from St. Louis Cathedral. She also ministered to condemned prisoners who at various times were ensconced within the confines of the Cabildo or on its grounds.

She performed litanies designed to free their tortured souls from the guilt and shame of their past and the fear and humiliation of their future. Many men died at the end of a rope with Marie's Ju-Ju beads in their mouths and her gris-gris bags in their trousers. The faith and love she provided these unfortunates were perhaps the only salvation they would ever taste.

The Morphogenic field created by her Magick still exists to this day. On the darkest night of the Lunar year it has been alleged that a vortex appears issuing from the Cabildo joining the worlds of light and darkness, life and death. Souls, shades, astral bodies, whatever one chooses to call them, have free access to our world; our world that crushed the life's breath from their quivering throats. On this night, it has been rumored that a great, black deamon rushes forth with gapping jaws and leopard's teeth to . . . .

Such is the hyperbolic balderdash which spews forth from the black garbed tour guides who are more interested in money and sensationalism than accurate historical research. Upon conducting several extensive interviews with employees of the

Illustrious Cabildo (which now houses part of the collections of Louisiana's past) as well as a critical search of the bibliographic record, this author could surface no substantiation of this site's

Classic Spanish Colonial Architecture

being haunted. Caveat Emptor!

Le Petit Theatre

Theaters are dream machines. Within their walls the fantastic becomes the mundane. It is here that the impossible is replaced by the probable and the expected is never what is found. Theaters are magical places where dreams come true and nightmares gallop to confrontation. Given this state of affairs it should come as no surprise to learn that many theaters have become the abodes of dark and mysterious forces.

Fact and fiction second this assertion. *The Phantom of the Opera*, *Poe's Masque of the Red Death*, both use theaters or theatrical motifs to introduce eldritch specters to an eager public. The infamous Ford's Theater in Washington, DC is reputed to entertain several ghosts. Less well known, but very benevolent are the ghosts which haunt The Wool Warehouse Theater Restaurant in Albuquerque, N.M., and The Grand Opera House in Oshkosh, Wisconsin. In both cases the ghosts display the utmost concern for their theaters and staffs (Myers, pp. 232-235 and pp. 350-354).

The literature, both fictional and factual, second the idea of theaters being haunted. Quite naturally, New Orleans has a theater attended by a family of ghosts.

Le Petit Theatre has been such since 1922. Before that it served a variety of commercial ventures. The building itself is numbered as among the first to be erected after the fire of 1795. As such, it is easily dated as Circa 1795.

It seems as though most of the ectoplasmic cast of Le Petit were, in life, participants in the theater's art. For example, we know of a young, married actress by the name of Caroline. One day while perfecting her craft, she met a fellow actor and fell deeply in love. Try as she may, she could not drive the thoughts of this man from her mind. Caroline blew lines. Her presence was eroding. The art that she held so dear was suffocating because of her unrequited love. After many torture-filled nights and tear-drenched days, she fell into the arms of her passion. She and the handsome thespian became lovers. He was also married, so their love-making nests were few in the days before motels and moral relativity.

Their favorite rendezvous was a little used storage room on the upper floor of the theater. It was here that they passed many evenings of joy and nights of bliss veiled by lies to their ever increasingly suspicious spouses.

The inevitable happened. Caroline's husband confronted her about his growing feelings of betrayal. In fear and shame, she fled her home for the only other comfort she had come to know—the theater. She searched stage left, stage right; the dressing rooms, prop rooms, offices—her love was nowhere to be found. Her last resort was the quarters that held them in the dark embrace where they shared each other and forgot the shackles of the world without. She entered the shadow-slashed chamber, heart thundering as she called her paramour's sweet name.

What happened next no one can say with certainty. What is known is that she plummeted through the cloudy window to meet death on the hard, cold, gray stones of the courtyard below. With her tragic demise her ghost was given birth. Here is the most active of the theater's ghosts. She has been observed by dozens of witnesses who feel her presence, her touch, her concern for those who share her abode. Caroline is an interactive ghost (see epilogue *New Orleans Ghosts*). The love and concern that was obvious in her life is preserved in her death. Caroline warns her living colleagues about possible dangers, and is instrumental in aiding them in the discovery of lost objects.

Stephen Thurber, former assistant technical director, is on record maintaining it is almost a tradition among the actors and staff to ask Caroline's help in finding lost items. Thurber related his own experience about his inability to surface several swords needed for an upcoming production. He searched everywhere; asked everyone. No luck! Futility more than reason now guided his actions as he asked for the good grace of our deceased actress in finding his needed weapons. After several minutes

The Scene of Much Romance

he felt drawn to a room he had searched previously. No sooner had he opened the door than his eyes reflected the bright steel for which he had rummaged so futilely.

As an interesting aside it should be remarked that the pre-Vatican II Roman Catholic Church had a similar custom involving St. Anthony of Padua (1195-1231). For generations the Catholic folk of New Orleans, for that matter Southern Louisiana, have made offerings to that vulnerable, old Franciscan monk in return for lost objects. I, personally, have tried it and it works an amazing amount of time! When you lose something, and it is impossible to find it, and you have exhausted all rational and intuitive avenues, then say a prayer something like this, *Oh, gracious St. Anthony, patron of the poor, and of those who seek lost objects, I humbly implore thee to return to me my misplaced Lear Jet. Upon its return I shall send you $1.00 for your beloved poor.*

Upon your lost possession's being restored, send $1.00 with a note saying, *For favors granted I give to St. Anthony of Padua $1.00 for his beloved poor.*

Sign and send it to: St. Anthony of Padua Church, 4640 Canal Street, New Orleans, LA 70119.

An unusual and unaccounted aspect of Caroline's haunting is that on numerous occasions she also appears in the company of groups of young, ghostly children who dance and sing around her ethereal gowns. Who these children might have been or their relationship to the deceased is without answer or conjecture.

A second haunting also centers around sex and death. An anonymous actress is rumored to have had a torrid love affair with one of the theater's early directors. As hard as this is to imagine our ingenue fell into the lustful deceit of this cad. He promised her choice parts and top billings for her exquisite favors. She obliged him while fantasies of fame, passion, acclaim, fortune played forth in her empty, beautiful head. His promises faded as fast as his favor. No part did she receive. No billing was hers.

Instead of fame, she gained infamy. The laughs and snickers did not pass unheeded. No acclaim, only ridicule preceded her. Humiliation became her shadow. Finally, it happened. A new play was cast. Her name was absent. She was given a schedule of future auditions, her pay, and escorted to the door.

Alone in her cramped, cheap room, the rivers of tears that flowed down her powdered cheeks collected into pools of vengeance. Her art crafted her response to the mortification that now pronounced her life. She planned well. She became both character and motivation for a part written by Shame.

On opening night she gained access backstage. A stagehand willingly allowed her freedom and privacy. She ascended to the catwalk above. She waited. Below she saw the director and his new love–the star of tonight's show. The scene below strengthened her resolve. It is she who should be the star tonight, and indeed, it would be!

As she watched the first act she whispered to herself, *God, this little whore is sooooo AFFECTED. Oh, and those God-damn pregnant pauses . . . for Pete's sake, everybody must know he's fuckin' her, 'cause she sure can't act.*

Acts two and three only reinforced her aesthetic critique. *Surely, everyone has to see that this is flop,* she muttered.

Curtain call. Now for the Play! She pinned up her chestnut colored hair. The noose slipped effortlessly around her thin, alabaster throat. She waited. The house lights blazed on. The curtain flew open. Applause thundered across the proscenium arch. Our heroine leaped into the void, leaped to fame and immortality! The hemp rope snapped taut after allowing a fourteen foot free fall. Not only did the rope snap, but so did her cervical vertebrae with such force that her gorgeous head was rent from her curvaceous, urine-soiled body. Her performance was unique.

It is her unhappy presence that generates feelings of uneasiness and sorrow at the foot of the stage. It is she whose betrayal creates a cold spot that cannot be resolved. It is she who is anonymous.

Also haunting these environs are two unlikely spectral legends. For many years the theater employed an old German carpenter, Sigmund. He was an able and conscientious worker. After his death his shade has appeared on numerous occasions, playing tricks and pranks that in life would never have crossed Sigmund's practical, artisan's mind.

When not perplexed by our sausage eater's gags some witnesses have been caught in the cold, emotionless stare of a man in white face and top hat who just sits in the empty audience space. When approached he vanishes. Like the children mentioned previously there is no accounting for his stark, lonely presence.

To conclude, I feel it is important to add an anecdote contributed by Mr. Thurber. He relates that he and two colleagues were searching the theater for some misplaced artifact. When he approached a particular room he was filled with feelings of foreboding and fear. His angst was such that he voiced to his companions his irrational fear. Only through shame and ridicule did he find the courage to open the door. Instantly a fuzzy human form exploded forward knocking Thurber to the floor. The figure vanished. Thurber discovered blood spewing from his nose and mouth. The two men with him were in a state of complete bewilderment.

Virtually all of the ghost legends I have investigated involving an interactive ghost (see Klein, pp. 107-114) indicated a benevolent, peaceful, sometimes playful spirit. It is indeed rare to surface any evidence about a malevolent revenent. I believe this is the case because whatever specie of life there is after death most assuredly retains the characteristics it manifested in *life*. I think that essentially most people are benevolent, kind and sometimes playful. What poisons us as a race are the tyrannical structures that we maintain to the detriment of our humanity. With death the ersatz structures of government, religion, ethics, morality, etc. assume their proper place—oblivion. In this world of shades illusion is cast aside and our only confrontation is with the self. Usually when this unencumbered self radiates into our world it is with bemused friendship.

The Witch of the
French Quarter Opera House

If love and betrayal are the mortar and stone of ghost legends then the sad story of Madame Marguerite Sauvé is the Home Depot for a strange, ethereal haunting that besieged the city exactly one hundred years ago. The Opera House that figures prominently in this story was destroyed by fire 4 December 1919. No cause has ever been established for the conflagration which destroyed it. Today, the site is occupied by the Downtowner Hotel. And all seems quiet.

Our story begins with the birth of Marguerite O'Donnell in 1842. She was the youngest of thirteen children born to a French mother and a newly arrived Irish immigrant father, Michael O'Donnell. She inherited her mother's French looks and her father's outgoing demeanor. Life was difficult, at best, for our charming young heroine. She married Octave Sauvé more for escape than for love. One year later, the Civil War raged. She lost all of her brothers and four of her brothers-in-law. Octave returned unscathed (de Lavigne, 1946, p. 167).

Her marriage was worse than her life as a virgin. Not only must she cook, clean and wash, but she was compelled to yield to the absinthe tainted embraces of her spouse. Her marriage was without issue. This fact contributed to Monsieur Sauvé's frustration. The marriage became a field of abuse. In 1875 at the age of thirty-three, Madame Sauvé sought release from her nightmare by pursuing a second, nocturnal life. She applied to

the French Opera House. She was accepted into the chorus.
Marguerite had little trouble hiding her new life from her
husband. Octave worked at night. His days were spent
sleeping or drinking. Sex with Marguerite had ceased. He
cared not at all for her barren pasture. Absinthe and opium
consumed his passions and frustrations.

Marguerite, now relatively free, fell easily into the gaiety of
the theater. She had friends; she had lovers; she had release
from the boredom and pain of her life.

The yellow fever epidemic of 1878 claimed the remainder of
her siblings and the hated Octave. She was free to indulge
herself in whatever her fading beauty could command. She
lived on her salary and the "donations" of gentlemen admirers.
As time past, so did the generosity of the fine young men in silk
hats with gold handled canes.

In the twilight of her beauty she began an affair with an
elderly gentlemen, a Monsieur de Boisblanc. Although now past
her forty-first year, Marguerite still retained a striking shadow of
her beauty. She also brought with her the skills and passions
she had acquired as a chorus girl. The relationship was
mutually beneficial. The old man gave her jewels and fine
clothes. She brought pleasure to his flickering life. In fact, she
brought so much pleasure to Monsieur de Boisblanc that he
died from exhaustion three months after his accomplished
mistress moved in. Apart from the expensive gifts she had
collected, her benefactor bequeathed her ten thousand dollars
in gold coins–a fortune in late nineteenth century America.

Madame proved to be a shrewd business person. She
opened Les Camellias which quickly became the most popular
confectioner in the French Quarter. Many of the patrons of the
French Opera House ended or sometimes began their night
sampling her exquisite delicacies. Fruit sherberts, puff tartes,
gateaux, glaces, dragées, méringues, darioles, pâtés brisées,
crème au vin, café au lait, chocolates all excited the palate at
Madame's Les Camélias. Her shop was known and enjoyed by
aristocrat and worker, actress and bon vivant, her success was
megalithic.

Madame attended her business dressed in elegant, yet
alluring, dark coiffes. Her jewelry, though understated was
elegant, refined. She fought back the years with treatments of

hot tallow and olive oil. Dye darkened her hair to the color of the raven's wing. Poudre Blanche and arsenic salts helped to hide and dissipate crow's feet and the furrows care had ploughed into her forehead. Madame knew she was aging, and her beauty just a flicker of its former glory. Nevertheless, she aged with grace and dignity. She also rested in the security of her thriving business and growing bank accounts. The hard life of her youth was gone with her beauty; however, she now enjoyed a life of respect and moderate wealth. She was content.

Her greatest problem sprung from the Victorian society of which she was a member. A successful businesswoman could be viewed with suspicion and contempt. Over the years she had employed four pastry chefs: Eugene, Victor, Francois and Septime. Each had tried assertions that wore Madame's patience. Each had eventually hinted at marriage; one even demanded it! Septime proved no better, no worse. She needed a husband. Someone to look out for her. A protector who would provide for her, *Mon Dieu*, she whispered to herself, *have I not heard this before, and to what avail*?

Madame advertised in the papers of Baltimore, Charleston, Savannah, Tampa, Mobile and Galveston (de Lavigne, 1946, p. 169). One morning her post contained a letter from one Carlos Alfaro of Tampa. He reported that he was twenty-one years of age; of Spanish lineage; possessed of a fine hand capable of many culinary delights. Carlos was also of a distinguished family capable of boasting that among its members was General Elroy Alfare, President of Ecuador (de Lavigne, 1946, p. 169). Remembered by history as Elroy the Eliminator, Elroy the Executioner, Elroy the Beast, etc., etc., etc.

Here was a young alarmingly young man who would no doubt be easy to control. She anticipated that her change in staff would only amount to a modest inconvenience. It was in this vein that she awaited the arrival of Carlos.

Septime became increasingly irritating. He had even been so bold as to comment on her poudres blanche et rouge. Madame knew his game all too well. He wanted her to be dependent on him. Then he could control her and her ever-growing wealth. Madame was aware of the ways of men. She had known them as father and brothers and she loved them. She also knew them as her caustic, bitter, broke husband and despised them. Marguerite had seen them all in her years as a chorus girl. She remembered the heady return to prosperity days after Reconstruction ended and the Federal troops withdrew. It was then in the spring of 1878 that she met Silas McIver of Irish descent as was she. Sy, as he was known, entered the US in 1859. In 1861 he accepted a $500 bounty to join the Union Army in the place of another. The $500 he invested in telegraph and railroad stock and marched off to war. By 1863 he was in New Orleans. Fortune smiled on him because when he was discharged in 1865 as a brevit major he was in a perfect position to take advantage of the city's fallen economy.

When Marguerite met him he was a successful hemp and indigo merchant with high-tech interests in telegraphs and railroads. He was tall and strong with crystal blue eyes and a mane of wavy ochre hair. From 1878 until the winter of 1880, Marguerite looked upon Sy as an operatic hero come to life–come to her life–to show her the New Orleans of Balls and Masques, of frivolity and license. For almost two glorious years she had a relationship that brought beauty and fulfillment to her otherwise barren existence. Colette de Bourbon, the very name brought gall to her tongue. She remembered the twenty-two-year-old blond slut and how Sy cast his pearls before the bitch. *Sacre bleu*, she shouted, as her conscious mind tore into the reality of her shop Les Camélias and her somewhat amused clientele.   Face blushing, she retreated to her quarters for privacy and laudanum.

Carlos' arrival was mundane. He reported to Les Camélias with two valises, a charming smile and the eyes of a fawn. Madame was immediately captivated by this boyish, Latin caballero.   Her heart raced; perspiration appeared on her forehead and the nape of her slender neck. Her eyes, pupils already dilated with belladonna, became bottomless black pools of passion as they feasted on the fantasy before her. Carlos did not fail to notice Madame's reactions.

Within a week, Marguerite discovered that Carlos had much to learn before he could be called a pastry chef. She felt it would be easier to teach him than apply for a replacement, and she loved being around him.

Marguerite realized that she thought of Carlos constantly. She tried to rationalize her obsession by dismissing it as simply a maternal instinct that had never been addressed. No! No! No! She knew this was a lie. She wanted him as a lover. Someone who could return to her the passion of her youth if not her youth itself. Mon Dieu, she was on fire.

The next day, an accidental close encounter in a pantry ended with dawn bidding adieu to a night of endless, forbidden passion. Her life now would be forever changed. Carlos was her paramour–her lover–her desire–her release.

Their love begot a new energy which channeled into everything. Her business, always prosperous, virtually doubled. Part of the income was due to the charm of handsome Carlos. His impeccable manners, easy charm and sincere ways earned him many friends and admirers, especially among the female gender. Madame watched him carefully for she knew the ways of men; however, her practiced, somewhat cynical eye found no deception in either his words or deeds.

Every evening upon closing they retired to madame's boudoir for hours of unrelenting sex. He was hers totally. One morning she informed him that he should take better care of his appearance. She prescribed that he acquire a new ensemble and present himself to a good barber for *a make over*. She notified the proper merchants and off he went. After nearly eight hours, Carlos returned to his benefactor. A beige linen suit draped his slim, muscular body. He wore a tasteful silk cravat and immaculate sky blue shirt. His feet were held by finely crafted, Italian shoes constructed of suede and vellum. As Madame kissed him, she smelled the crispness of witch hazel and the murky sensuality of violet oil. They made love for hours.

As the weeks expanded so did her generosity or perhaps her gratefulness. Carlos was granted a small suite at a local upscale hotel. His salary was $125 a week when a good wage in 1900 was $12.50 per. Madame allowed Carlos a three-day work week. Everything was for Carlos!

One crisp, cool night after a marathon of sex, Carlos, exhausted and flush with absinth and bitters, made the fatal error of babbling in his stupor, *Oh, Lisette, Lisette, I love you so much. . . not like that old sow, Marguerite . . . Oh, Lisette. . . .*

Madame was incensed.   She planned her vengeance carefully. Marguerite had the means to learn every detail of the life Carlos led when not in her company. What she learned brought her much sorrow. Lisette was young, beautiful. She was also a drug addicted whore. At times her favors were as cheap as a glass of absinthe or a draught of laudanum. Carlos met her three months before at the Olde Absinthe House. Since then he had rented her rooms on Saint Ann near Royal. He also used Madame Sauvé's silver to purchase a dozen pairs of silk hose, a silk robe, fur and oriental rugs, five bottles of imported parfume, acres of silk, satin, lace, linen and assorted other finery (de Lavigne, 1946, p. 172). The thought of her money supporting Lisette Leboeuf, a strumpet, brought her an ecstatic orchestra of humiliation, anger and hate!

One morning she awoke to find Carlos absent. This was her chance. She armed herself as her passion demanded. She proceeded to the French Opera House for reasons known only to her. From her meditation she preceded to the whore's residence. She ascended the stairs; her thoughts her only accomplice. Outside of Lisette's door, Madame froze. Her ears seemed to be her only sense. She listened for love; for moans; for betrayal. Silence emboldened her. Her hand found the door unlocked. With a spider's stealth she entered Lisette's domain. Incense and opium slept in the still air. She walked across the parlor to the half-closed door which she instinctively knew hid Lisette's boudoir. Marguerite's heart thundered. She peered into the dark, moist embrace of the room. There before her tear weary eyes were the naked bodies of Carlos and Lisette exhausted by their erotic ballet. Marguerite crept toward the couple hoping the sound of her heart would not arouse them from the arms of Hypnos. A thousand thoughts stampeded across her mind like armed vandals. They must die! But, How, How?   She wanted to decapitate them—eviscerate them—immolate them–but then a finer thread of vengeance wove its web.

Hapless Madame remembered the occult rituals of Voo-Doo she had seen as a child. Conversations with her hair dresser, Marie Laveau leaped from her memory. Her retribution, her justice would rise from her grave. She knew how to do it. First, she must find some personal item that linked Carlos and Lisette through love. Jewelry perhaps? No, how could she be sure it was the bounty of Carlos' love and not of another paramour? Her fingers and eyes danced across the room to the accompaniment of the rhythmic sounds of slumber dripping from the bed which embraced Carlos and Lisette. A letter! She found a letter! It was a love letter from her beloved Carlos to his strumpet Lisette. The perfect vehicle for a sympathetic link with the world of mystery.   Letter in trembling hands, she approached the dissipated lovers. She smeared the letter with the still moist body fluids clinging to the satin sheet. Then she pierced her finger and trailed a line of blood across the fine, linen surface of the document. The letter was then bisected and each half bound with a black ribbon from our heroine's dress. One portion was concealed behind a loose brick in the fire place. The other accompanied her to fulfill her occult purposes.

She repaired to her rooms where she changed her will leaving Carlos nothing, and wrote a suicide note. The note declared her intention of ending her life, and that no one was to blame. The note also affirmed that she would return in order to finish a task best left to the dead (de Lavigne, 1946, p. 175).

This business executed she then trudged to the opera house where she could find the tools necessary for the ritual that would begin her journey into darkness. Here she found the privacy to assemble the dagger, sword, charcoal, cloth, nails, etc. needed for her work. The ritual concluded when Madame concealed her half of the letter of betrayal in a cobweb-insulated cranny in the rafters above the stage. She returned home to send a bullet through her skull.

Scandal, rumor, speculation spewed throughout the city. No quarter was so dismayed as Carlos and Lisette's. Their meal ticket had been canceled. Carlos prepared to weather the storm by scraping up enough money to pay his and Lisette's rent for two months while he hunted for new employment—or a new benefactress.

The storm was of short duration for the licentious duo. Three days after Madame's funeral, around midnight, a witness claimed to have seen a translucent, white form emerge form the Old French Opera House. The shade glided down Bourbon to Toulouse, then to Royal where it navigated around the corner of

Saint Ann. The ghost vanished at the entrance to Carlos and Lisette's apartment (de Lavigne, 1946, p. 176).

The next morning, tenants were alarmed by the smell of gas. The fire department was alerted. Upon entering the toxic rooms they found our lovers–dead. Their faces were frozen masks of terror. A coroner's inquest judged the incident to be suicide, discounting the story of a ghost, as related by a witness, to be alcohol induced.

Interestingly enough, whenever a new tenant took occupancy of the rooms, neighbors and passers-by again echoed the story of that original witness. This phenomenon was so consistent that everyone knew the story and began calling the revenent the *Witch of the French Opera House.*

4 December 1919 a new tenant, cleaning her new apartment found half of an old love letter written in a fine, flowing hand. She tossed the paper into the crackling fire of her fire place. Instantly the infamous witch appeared moaning and weeping and reaching futilely vainly for the scrap of paper, but, alas, the flames had already done their work. The pale shape mirrored the destruction of the parchment and followed the white ash up the chimney never to be seen again.

It should also be noted that on that same evening the French Opera House was completely consumed by flames of a completely mysterious origin (Huber, p. 158)

Delta Queen

The introduction of Mr. Fulton's folly to the Mississippi River brought New Orleans even greater riches and romance. Riverboats plied the murky waters beginning in 1812 with the arrival of the single cylinder "New Orleans" (Taylor, pp. 70-71).

Steamboats were soon traveling hotels transporting people in luxury and goods with relative safety and speed. By 1830, the great boats came and went with each hour (Leavitt, p. 80). Legends and myths clung to the hulls of the mighty river queens. Their names rang with majesty and honor: The American, Valley Queen, Belle of Memphis, Sultana, Silver Wave, Mayflower and the fabled Natchez and Robert E. Lee among others.

Their contributions to commerce and culture were immortalized by Mark Twain, Davey Crockett, Mike Fink and a host of other literati and ruffians. The steamboat contributed to the westward expansion of America and left an indelible mark on its colorful, somewhat brutal history. These magnificent vessels are immortalized on currency, in poems and in the imagination of countless souls who have witnessed their transits on rivers and throughout history.

After the Civil War, which was anything but civil, the majestic boats powered by steam fell victim to another nineteenth century marvel–the Railroad. During the administration of Abraham Lincoln, the concept of a transcontinental railroad was birthed. By 1869, the project found fruition at Promitory Point,

Utah. The steam engine began to replace the steamboat. It was faster. More efficient. Death knells shattered the air of the elegant queens of the dark ribbons of river that breathed vitality into America's expansion. By the close of the previous century the lovely paddle wheels faced extinction. Their sun had set. Commerce found a new whore. The frontier became a memory. Romance vanished.

The twentieth century dawned with an explosion of technology and bloodletting unparalleled in time. Steamboats became scrap. Nevertheless, there were some who cherished the memory and heritage of those grand water castles.

Gordon C. Green was one such person. During the 1890s, he founded the Delta Queen Steamboat Co. He acquired the steamship H. K. Bedford and began cruises for the public. At this time he also acquired a wife, Mary Becker, of Marietta, Ohio. Mrs. Green loved the grand old river dames. She learned everything she could about the boats and the river. Currents, depths, pistons and pipes all became second nature to her. By 1895 she became one of a handful of women to earn a coveted pilot's license. Within a few years she was Captain Mary—a full-fledged riverboat captain. Mary's love of the river was passed onto her two boys, Tom and Chris. This was a river boat family. Mr. And Mrs. Green had their quarters on board. The couple lived, loved, dreamed and grew old gliding up and down that mighty Mississippi.

Their business thrived. Their children reached maturity. In 1927, Gordon died, but his dream did not. Mary and her sons proudly captained their growing fleet of luxury passenger boats. Captain Mary was the River Mother. Although a pragmatic business woman, accomplished pilot and worldly person, she was also a loving, caring soul. She married her loving personhood to her family which was extended to include all whom her broad, smiling face encountered. She cared for the dark river. She cared for all who rode that artery of America's life and commerce. She cared!

The apogee of Mary's aspirations came to fruition in 1946 when her son, Tom Green, purchased the Delta Queen. Here was the culmination of her dreams in a *Flag Ship*. The beautiful Queen, built in 1926, saw a variety of services, including a stint with the U. S. Army during the bedlam and terror of World War

II. Her purchaser subjected her to renovations which totaled $750,000. The Delta Queen became a true Queen with all the royalty and beauty of aristocracy in a world that prized democracy but longed for the delicate beauty of privilege. An oxymoron relinquished by Washington but maintained in the psyche of America.

Captain Mary's fifty-five year reign ended April 1949. Mary's life was fulfilled by the river even in death. She was a respected River Pilot, business person, wife and mother who preserved history and beauty with her existence.

According to a variety of reasonable witnesses, Mary's love of the River and her beloved boats were not to be dimmed by death's gray eye. Her benevolent shade has been reported numerous times. Mike Williams, the Delta Queen's first mate, was sleeping in his quarters. Around 1:45 A.M. his peace was disturbed by hot breath on his neck. He thought it a dream and began to return to the embrace of his dark bed. Again he was startled, this time to vigilant consciousness. Believing an intruder had gained access to the moored vessel, he investigated gingerly. Upon entering the engine room he heard the unmistakable sound of rushing water. A rusted pipe had burst. He made the necessary repairs. Had not Williams been awakened, the damage would almost certainly have sent the Delta Queen to a watery grave.

Shortly after this incident the purser, Myra Frougeat, received a complaint from cabin 512. The party on the other end of the line sounded like an elderly woman. Myra hung up the receiver and immediately called the first mate to report the problem. While waiting for Williams, Ms. Frougeat looked up from her desk. She saw an old lady smiling at her through the window. She returned the smile. Her visitor then seemed to vanish.

All of the above was related to Williams. He proceeded to investigate the complaint. He knocked on the door of room 512. No response. Again he knocked and inquired verbally. Fearing the worst he used his pass key to gain entrance. No one was in the room. Mike returned to the purser and asked her further questions which resolved nothing. Later that evening Williams escorted Myra to her cabin. As they were walking down the hall Myra commented that the woman she saw in the window was the same woman whose photographs were in the lounge.

Williams informed her that those photographs were of Captain Mary who died in 1949. Mike and Myra, soon after that incident, began to grow increasingly fond of one another. Their fondness developed into love and they were married.

When Mike and Myra talk about their marriage they tell people they were introduced by Captain Mary Green.

Captain Mary is a benevolent ghost. She cares for her ships and the people who operate them. The love she expressed in life continues after her death.

Those uncommon instances when a ghost is malevolent I believe point to part of a continuing pathology that has yet to find resolution and enlightenment on the other side.

Potter's Field

New Orleans is renowned for her cemeteries. St. Louis I, II, and III, Metairie, Lafayette, St. Roch cemeteries each draws thousands of tourists, historians, mourners and initiates. Very few residents are familiar with Holt Cemetery located on General Diaz and Virginia Streets.

Holt was chartered in 1879. Its grounds were reserved for the indigent. No confederate generals nor governors are held by its damp, verdant soil. Here are the remains of transients, whores, the poor, the homeless, the unclaimed. We find drunkards, addicts, the unknown and forgotten. Occasionally, the eye will find a veteran's headstone with name, rank and serial number. By and large the yard is forested with planks, or ironing boards bearing hand scratched information.

Part of the original charter mandated that Holt would be a resting place for paupers. One's body would remain in a plot as long as the deceased significant others maintained the tiny property. When obvious maintenance stopped the remains would be obliged to share with the new occupant as the resident du jour complete with a new plank or board or whatever. As a consequence this relatively small graveyard holds tens of thousands of corpses. It is not unusual for one to stroll among the oaks and clover to discover skulls and jaw bones, thighs and vertebrae. Because of this grisly bounty legends of ghouls haunt Holt searching for bones to be used in the many occult rituals held throughout the city on any given night.

Mrs. A. J., a neighbor of the cemetery, whose windows overlook Holt related the following: *It be worstest on Hally Ween. Dem's people come on up ir d'er an boun candils an kill chickens and mices and stuff. Den d'ey has sex. Oh, Lawd strike me if'n I lyin' yes, sir, dat's wha dey dooo!*

Ya goes in d'ere sometimes too ya hear noises, but nuthin' d'ere, ya understan'? I ain't never seen no ghostez but ya understan I heared stuff and I seen dem devil worshippers ya understand wha' I sayin?

The author is aware of an occultist G. R. who visits Holt with his acolytes on the nights of the four ancient, Celtic fire rituals. He reported that if one is diligent body parts can be uncovered–especially after heavy rains.

Perhaps the most obvious spirit in residence of the neglected necropolis is Polyhymnia the Muse of Sacred Poetry.In death's forsaken spur the Human Spirit of Art reigns with the majestic oaks and the conqueror worm. With fleeting expressions of macabre creativity those who remain on this bank of the river Styx have left Art to comfort their dead. On a time-tattered grave a laboratory quality gram scale stands vigil.

Photographed as Found

Stones and shells and shattered glass merge into geometrical patterns that fire refracted light toward the blue abyss above. Crude, fading images of the dearly departed reflect the rotting masks which lie beneath them.

The grandeur of Metairie is not here. The decadent decay of the St. Louis trinity is here not apparent; however, the Spirit of Humanity resides in all of its glory and triumph for those who

Ironing Board Marker

wish to take the time to see!

The Haunted House of Lakeview

N ight has fallen like a gallows trap. Shattering glass punctuates the relentless screams and howls that rip across the shadowy, star stained darkness. A black stone house of irregular shape holds the emaciated, pale forms of a small family imprisoned by fear, and the unyielding vengeance of the phantoms who roam at will across their property. Inside the vine-covered edifice, crisscrossed with zigzag fissures, an elderly father sits motionless, riveted by desperation. Two daughters, Rebecca and Martha, huddle in a dark corner clutching each other and whatever remains of their sanity. Years before, in 1930, the old man's only son was committed to the state's mental hospital–a stark-raving lunatic beyond human aid or comfort.

This unfolding human tragedy began in 1927 when Paul Orchard, the patriarch of the besieged clan, built his home. Orchard was an eccentric man. His fear of fire compelled him to build his house of stone and concrete with an asbestos roof. Doors were the only wood in the entire structure. Each room held a private bathroom. Orchard designed and built his retreat singlehandedly. Finishing in 1929, he returned to his home state of Florida to retrieve his children (Kieth, p. 119).

Old Paul was estranged from his wife. She and her family spirited the children away to an unknown location and began the exquisitely sadistic process of poisoning their malleable minds against their father. After a villainous separation, Paul and his family were at war with his wife Estelle, and her matriarchal, dominating flock.

The children, an unnamed son (b. 1919?), Martha (b. 1921) and Rebecca (b. 1923), were not normal. Paul's son was mentally challenged with psychotic episodes. The poor creature never progressed past being an undomesticated beast. No doubt his condition was exacerbated by unhygienic psychological experiences in his formative years.

Martha was shy, retiring but friendly and amazingly well adjusted considering the pathology to which she was exposed. She and her siblings were kidnaped regrettably by two warring tribes lead by Paul and Estelle. Intrigue, fear, hate, passion rode across the children's frontiers as if in some apocalyptic nightmare.

Rebecca did not fare well. She played with dolls her entire life. At the time of her death, in 1976, in the same insane asylum that muffled her brother's death some four decades past she possessed an astoundingly dirty, valuable collection. The perverted passions of her family had victimized her by a deamon that surpassed any Satan.

This was the Orchard clan. Martha attended the local schools and was reported to be kind, but reserved (Keith). Paul was a recluse. Rebecca and *Junior* were never seen. They belonged to the Methodist church and attended services. All through the Great Depression, the family was considered peculiar but respectable.

No one is sure when *It* began. Some swear *It* began in the early days of WW II. Others affirm *It* became manifest during Eisenhower's reign of peace and prosperity. Whatever! An evil came into being that tormented the hapless homeowners until death released them from their agonies.

For years neighbors benignly referred to the bizarre, sinking, stone building as *The Palace*. Suddenly, after years of passive indifference, Papa Paul's palace became the sphincter for humanity's most repulsive excreta.   Youthful night riders descended upon the home.   Harpies hurled bottles. Succubuses slung shit. Incubi intimidated and isolated with obscene insults.

The Orchards, incapable of terminating the assaults, withdrew into a cocoon of depravity. Night following night the vandals plied their trade. Windows were shattered. In one year the old man replaced 63 panes of glass. Halloween and New Years were worst. Gangs of ghouls would assemble on the curb to release fusillades of fireworks at the besieged bunker of blasphemy. Dry flora ignited. Doors smoldered. Windows were raped by rockets and pyrotechnics that brought light and fire into the dark recesses of Orchard's trembling domain.

During 1973, Paul expired. He was buried in the Methodist church wearing his trademark red flannel shirt. His varied bank accounts yielded $93,000. Martha was executor of the estate. She invested equally in CD's and stocks.

The raids from hell persisted. Shattering an assumed, peaceful night, howls, curses slashed sleep, freedom. The sisters checked bolted doors frantically, called the police. Virtually every night was spent clutching each other; praying for cessation, an end.

Several days before Christmas 1974 a neighbor crouched under Martha's bedroom window and called her name. Martha answered her inquiry. Terrified, Martha affirmed her well being. Christmas Eve brought with it the pungent odor of death. A forlorn Methodist minister answered the call. He and several neighbors forced the side door. Decay tore at their nostrils. Within the crumbling castle they discovered Rebecca. An iron bed rusted with continual floods of urine supported her ulcer infested flesh. The woman was in a state of severe malnutrition. She was irreversibly psychotic.

Dozens of cats had left decades of urine and feces. The house was awash with empty food cans and bottles. Legions of cockroaches competed with a rainbow of flies for filth. The symphony of odors created a triumphal march of olfactory obscenity sans pareil. Piles of rotting newspapers, soiled clothing and disabled furniture completed the decor (Keith).

The final discovery revealed Rebecca's corpse. Cats had feasted on her face, fingers and toes. Maggots poured from her private orifices. The minister and neighbors were replaced by police, medical personnel, the coroner. Martha was remanded to a mental hospital. Rebecca was removed to the morgue.

The court investigated their assets. CD's, stocks and bank accounts totaled $300,000. A hoard of coins and cash added $200,000 to the pot. The house and grounds upped the ante

$150,000. In total, Martha in her madness, possessed almost $700,000.

Who were the demons who descended upon the reeking, crooked house? What dark force unleashed them to bring hell calling on the Orchard family? Who? What? Why?

The phantoms who preyed upon the besieged clan were not a unique manifestation. They exist in towns and villages, cities and hamlets worldwide. These fiends justify their predation by labeling their victims as witches, ghouls, vampires, queers, etc. The deamons who drove the Orchards to despair and insanity are our children. They are us!

The Phantom and the Ax

Ever since Lizzie Borden took an ax (4 August 1893) and

> *. . . gave her mother forty wacks,*
> *When she saw what she had done*
> *She gave her father forty-one*

American culture has had a fascination for this particularly heinous form of homicide. Betty Davis in *Hush, Hush Sweet Charlotte*, then Joan Crawford in *Straightjacket* allowed the media to pay tribute to our vicarious relationship with the ax murderer.

Not to be outdone by these factual and fictional occurrences, the City that Care Forgot offers a unique addition to the menu. During the years of 1918 and 1919 the residents of the Crescent City were gripped by terror generated by one of history's most prolific and sadistic serial killers.

In the Spring of 1918, New Orleanians were concerned with the events of World War I and the encroaching tyranny of the Volstead Act as were most other Americans. Soon they would be haunted by a deamon whose lust for murder and sex would displace any international or national concerns.

It began with a headline in *The Times-Picayune* (24 May 1918) that announced a gruesome double murder. Mr. and Mrs. Joseph Maggio, proprietors of a small grocery store located at Upperline and Magnolia Streets, were brutally murdered. Both were slaughtered in their bed by an ax wielding maniac who finished his grisly work by also using a straight razor to cut their throats. The police were confronted by a scene of rare carnage. The bedroom was awash in blood and tissue. The floor and bed clothes were a crimson scandal.   Mr. and Mrs. Maggio's mutilated skulls had all but been removed from their bodies by the brutal slashings of the straight razor.

The police investigation revealed that the intruder chiseled out a small panel in the back door. There was no indication of robbery. Jewelry and several hundred dollars in cash were untouched by the villain. The blood-drenched ax and razor were left in plain sight on the back steps. Both were identified as property of the Maggios.   The house contained no fingerprints nor clues that could help surface the killer. The only evidence, if it could be called such, was the discovery of a cryptic message scrawled in chalk about a block away: "Mrs. Maggio is going to sit up tonight just like Mrs. Toney" (Tallant, 1952, p. 194).

Investigators tied this clue to a string of unsolved murders which plagued the city in 1911.   During this time, five individuals, all Italian grocers and their wives, had fallen victim to an identical, brutal attack. The first victim was a man named Cruti, then Mr. and Mrs. Rosetti, and finally Mr. and Mrs. Tony Schiambra. It was these last victims who linked these murders to those of the Maggios. Because of their nationality, the Mafia and the Black Hand were suspected; however, no arrests were made and the cases remained unsolved.

The police in their usual rush to injustice attempted to solve the Maggio murders by framing Mr. Maggio's innocent brothers Andrew and Jake.   The brothers shared a double with the unfortunate couple. They discovered the bodies. Such was enough for the cops to *solve* the case by condemning two innocent men. Within days the traumatized men were released due to lack of evidence, lack of motive, lack of opportunity, etc.

28 June 1918, John Zanca, a delivery man on his rounds, made a startling discovery. At a grocery owned by a Polish immigrant, Louis Besumer, the ax manic struck again, this time at a non-Italian businessman. Besumer and his mistress were both brutally attacked in their sleep. The Pole survived. Harriet Lowe was not so lucky; however, before she died she supplied the police with a description: a large, muscular, white male.

She described him further as wearing a hat or cap, a white shirt opened at the throat and short brown hair that seemed to stand straight up (Tallant, 1952).

That same night tragedy armed with an ax struck again. A pregnant woman, Mrs. Schneider, was discovered by Edward, her husband, upon his return from work. She had been savagely attacked. The trauma was so intense that the poor woman remembered nothing of the attack except a vague, dark form.

Upon investigation, the police discovered that the sadist, if it was he, had changed his modus operandi. The perpetrator had entered through a window, not a chiseled back door panel. No ax nor other weapons were found. Also, the attack left no dead. Both Mrs. Schneider and her fetus survived.

All of this not withstanding, Louis Besumer was again victimized. This time it was the police. He was arrested and charged with his paramour's murder even though she described someone else. (Off-duty police officers could easily acquire second jobs working for the railroad.)

10 August 1918, eighteen-year-old Pauline Bruno and her thirteen-year-old sister, Mary, were awakened by the sounds of a scuffle spilling out of their uncle's room. Investigating, they saw a *dark, tall, heavy-set (man), wearing a dark suit and a black slouch hat* assaulting Joseph Romano, their uncle. The figure literally vanished before their eyes (Tallant, 1952, p. 200).

Pauline later related the following to the *Item.*

> *I've been nervous about the Axman for weeks,* she said, *and I haven't been sleeping much. I was dozing when I heard blows and scuffing in Uncle Joe's room. I sat up in bed and my sister woke up too. When I looked into my uncle's room this big heavy-set man was standing at the foot of his bed. I think he was a white man, but I couldn't swear to it. I screamed. My little sister screamed too. We were horribly scared. Then he vanished. It was almost as if he had wings!*
> *We rushed into the parlor, where my uncle had staggered. He had two big cuts on his head. We got him up and propped him in a chair. I've been hit, he groaned. I don't know who did it.*

Call the Charity Hospital.   Then he fainted.
Later he was able to walk to the ambulance with
some help.   I don't know that he had any
enemies.

Two days after the attack Romano expired without having regained consciousness. All of the axman's signatures were on this murder however. A rear door panel was chiseled out. Romano's own ax was found in his back yard. The only remarkable deviation from the norm was that Uncle Joe was a barber, not a grocer.

The city's Italian community was rife with rumor and ablaze with anger and vigilance. Armed men patrolled the Italian community. Homes and businesses were barred and made more secure. Some families even moved out of town to weather the storm. A Joseph Garry vowed he leveled a shotgun blast at the axman to no avail. A grocer by the name of Joseph LeBeouf reported a chiseled rear door panel and ax on his property (Tallant, 1952, p. 201).

A report from *The New Orleans States-Item* declared:

Armed men are keeping watch over their sleeping
families while the police are seeking to solve the
mysteries of the ax attacks.   Five victims have
fallen under the dreadful blows of this weapon
within the last few months. Extra police are being
put to work daily.

At least four persons saw the Axman this morning
in the neighborhood of Iberville and Rendon. He
was first seen in front of an Italian grocery. Twice
he fled when citizens armed themselves and gave
chase.   There was something, agreed all, in the
prowler's hand. Was it an ax? . . . (Tallant, 1952,
p. 201-202)

Joseph Dantonio, an expert criminologist who had retired from the Detective Division of the NOPD was quoted by a reporter from *The States,*

The Axman is a modern "Dr. Jekyll and Mr. Hyde."
A criminal of this type may be a respectable, law-
abiding citizen when his normal self. Compelled by
an impulse to kill, he must obey this urge. Some
years ago there were a number of similar cases, all

bearing such strong resemblance to this outbreak that the same fiend may be responsible. Like Jack-the-Ripper, this sadist may go on with his periodic outbreaks until his death. For months, even for years, he may be normal, then go on another rampage. It is a mistake to blame the Mafia. Several of the victims have been other than Italians, and the Mafia never attacks women, as this murderer has done. (Tallant, 1952, p. 202)

There was a lull in the axman's activities until 10 March 1919. On that propitious day an Italian grocer, Ionlando Jordano, responded to cries emanating from the home of Charles Cortimiglia, a neighboring grocer. Entering the Cortimiglias' quarters he beheld a mutilated family. Charles suffered wounds to his face and arms. His lacerated jaw and destroyed teeth were fields of pain he would harvest until his death, 4 August 1929. Mrs. Cortimiglia's skull was held in place by blood soaked mats of hair and strands of skin that had avoided the fury of the ax. The private entrances and exits to her body had been violated in the most obvious and obscene manner. Most heartbreaking was the pitiful, convulsing body of two-year-old Mary. She shared her mother's condition!

Jordano's son Frank aided his father in giving first aid and summoning the proper authorities. All were rushed to Charity Hospital. Young Mary was pronounced D.O.A. Cortimiglia and daughter were in critical condition.

Again, the axman's modus operandi was obvious. There were no clues save for the statements made later by the recuperating couple. Charles described a large, white man to which Rosie, his wife, added dark clothes and tall stature. The police knew this was the general description offered by other victims and witnesses. 11 March 1919 the newspapers announced,

The Axeman Returns . . . Axeman Strikes Again

Several days after these revelations Rosie Cortimiglia changed her story completely. She accused her alleged rescuers as her alleged assailants. Her husband denied his wife's allegations and stood by his original statement that he had no knowledge of his attackers' identity. The city was in shock!

> *You mean the axeman is a sixty-nine years old*
> *Italian grocer and his nineteen- year-old son?*

Father and son, protesting their innocence, were arrested and imprisoned in the old Gretna jail on the Westbank of the Mississippi River. Their lawyers argued that the Jordanos could not have been *The Axman*, nor did they commit murder only to try to save their victims. Also, Mr. Cortimiglia was tearfully adamant that his assailant was a lone, white male of large build. He also stated that his wife was not responsible for what she said due to her many traumas. Not withstanding, *The People* elected to try the old man and his son for murder, among other charges, in May 1919.

It is important to reflect on this case as it has so far developed. We have a sadistic killer whose career has spanned nine years and eleven victims. He acquired his weapons from his victims. He is described as a large, robust white male wearing dark clothing. No one can describe him other than in generalities. No clues have surfaced, and the attacks are without obvious motive—no robbery, no link with one another, etc., etc. Also of note was an experiment done by the police. Assuming that the description of a tall, husky man could be matched minimally by a six foot, two-hundred pound individual such a person could have in no way squeezed through the panels removed from the various victims' homes. Also were the disturbing reports of his vanishing or completely disappearing.

Finally, why were five innocent men, some of whom victims, arrested, charged and in two cases convicted of murder? Could the police have been so unjust or so stupid as to brutalize so many obviously innocent men? Was there a cover-up of some sort? And if so, what could justify the attacks upon children and a pregnant women? Perhaps there is an occult or hidden aspect to so many miscarriages of justice during the police investigation.

Could it be that the belligerent phantom was also a type of psychic vampire who could project his malevolent thoughts to direct the actions of those he vexes? After all, the city was swallowed by paranoia in the wake of his killings. Perhaps he could somehow channel this energy to confound the police and stir negative emotions of fear and panic to the boiling point. If such a scenario is correct then what sort of an entity is this midnight-clad marauder? Maybe he, himself tells us in a letter he penned.

Hell, March 13, 1919

Editor of the Times-Picayune
New Orleans, Louisiana

Esteemed Mortal:
They have never caught me and they never will. They have never seen me, for I am invisible, even as the ether that surrounds your earth. I am not a human being, but a spirit and a fell demon from the hottest hell. I am what you Orleanians and your foolish police call the Axeman.
When I see fit, I shall come again and claim other victims. I alone know who they shall be. I shall leave no clue except my bloody ax, besmeared with the blood and brains of him whom I have sent below to keep me company.
If you wish you may tell the police not to rile me. Of course I am a reasonable spirit. I take no offense at the way they have conducted their investigations in the past. In fact, they have been so utterly stupid as to amuse not only me, but His Satanic Majesty, Francis Josef, etc. But tell them to beware. Let them not try to discover what I am, for it were better that they were never born than to incur the wrath of the Axeman. I don't think there is any need of such a warning, for I feel sure the police will always dodge me, as they have in the past. They are wise and know how to keep away from all harm.
Undoubtedly, you Orleanians think of me as a most horrible murderer, which I am, but I could be much worse if I wanted to. If I wished, I could pay a visit to your city every night. At will I could slay thousands of your best citizens, for I am in close relationship to the Angel of Death.

Now, to be exact, at 12:15 (earthly time) on next Tuesday night, I am going to visit New Orleans again. In my infinite mercy, I am going to make a proposition to you people. Here it is:

I am very fond of jazz music, and I swear by all the devils in the nether regions that every person shall be spared in whose home a jazz band is in full swing at the time I have mentioned. If everyone has a jazz band going, well, then, so much the better for you people. One thing is certain and that is that some of those people who do not jazz it on Tuesday night (if there be any) will get the ax.

Well, as I am cold and crave the warmth of my native Tartarus, and as it is about time that I leave your earthly home, I will cease my discourse. Hoping that thou wilt publish this, that it may go well with thee, I have been, am and will be the worst spirit that ever existed either in fact or realm of fancy.

The Axeman

(Talent, 1952, p. 207)

At least the axman had a sense of fair play. His appreciation of jazz and absurdity prompted New Orleanians to initiate axman parties and to even publish a musical tribute to the deamon titled, *The Mysterious Axman's Jazz*. The appointed date 19 March came and went without incident.

Back to the trials. Before Papa Jordano and his son were tried, Louis Besumer appeared before the Bar to answer to the murder of his mistress, Mrs. Lowe. District Attorney Chandler Luzenburg presented a weak case. The jury, after ten minutes of deliberation, returned a not guilty verdict.

The Jordanos were not so fortunate. Their trial, 21 May 1919, was a spectacle. The only witness against them was Rosie Cortimiglia. She was refuted by witness after witness including her own husband. Nothing, character witnesses, lack of weapons or evidence, expert witnesses could sway the jury. Frank was sentenced to be hanged. His father was remanded to serve a life term.

10 August Steve Boca stumbled from his Elysian Fields Avenue home carrying dreadful ax wounds on his skull. He

repaired to the home of his friend Frank Genusa about half a block away. Genusa treated his friend as best he could and then summoned help. The police found at Boca's home the classical axman M.O. chiseled door panel. Bloody ax, his property, left on premises. No theft. They immediately arrested Frank Genusa. Within a short period after his recovery Boca defended his friend to the overanxious *People*. Genusa was released.

2 September William Carson, a local druggist, fired several shots at an intruder. The police found all of the axman's calling cards: chiseled rear door panel, ax, no theft. By some quirk of fate the police failed to arrest Carson.

3 September a fair, nineteen-year-old girl was sleeping peacefully. She lived alone and was employed. From the deep velvet blackness of slumber and dreams an ax cleaved her bliss. Neighbors found the tragic Sarah Laumann clinging to life with bloodstained hands. Teeth, tissue and blood painted her bed with terror and pain. She lived; however, the memory of that night was gone with her beauty.

27 October Mrs. Mike Pepitone investigated a disturbance in her husband's private room. Her husband had been monstrously assailed. The Blessed Virgin Mary's statue had been desecrated by blood and brain matter. Mike was dead.

Again the axman's M.O. The authorities were baffled; the citizenry outraged. Editorials clamored for *Justice*, *Protection*, *Accountability*. Armed men roamed the streets. Families cowered behind bolted shutters and doors. *The* topic of conversation was the *Axman*.

> *Was there one axman or several?*
> *Why have the police no substantial leads nor evidence?*
> *Could this be a ghost or deamon as the letter confessed?*

Of course the populus had no way of knowing that this was the last appearance of the axman. No curtain calls. No more sightings. Nothing. The axman and his malevolence vanished as abruptly as they appeared. The police had made no valid arrests. Had no substantial evidence, clues. Descriptions, though consistent, were vague, ephemeral. He had killed and mutilated many citizens. Men, women and children witnessed no discrimination in this democratic deamon's eyes.

Public opinion was in an uproar. If the Jordanos, convicted on the testimony of a mentally unstable witness, were the *axman* then why did the *axman* continue to butcher?

William F. Byrnes, attorney of record for the convicted men, with the backing of most of the Gretna residents, readied briefs for the Supreme Court, and put pressure on Rosie.

7 December 1920 Rosie presented herself to the city room of *The Times-Picayune* and made a dramatic confession of perjury, vengeance, hatred and heartfelt remorse. She also reported that God through Saint Joseph had vested smallpox upon her for her mortal sins. She and her husband had been estranged since before the so-called trial.

The Jordanos were quickly exonerated and released to the joyful bosom of their family. Frank married almost immediately. Papa Jordano died soon after.

Could this monster have been something other than human? It is tempting to credit these unsolved, closed cases to an arcane species of supernormal event. Who or what forces held New Orleans in the sweaty palm of horror will more than likely never be known. The story has become a *spirit* in and of itself. It is part of a unique truth/folklore that appeals to the imagination. As such, it shall stimulate thought and sustain culture.

Addendum: A fact (possibly salient; possibly coincidental) was brought to the attention of the NOPD. The LAPD reported than an Orleanian, one Joseph Mumpre, had been gunned down by a *woman in black and heavily veiled* . . . (Talent, 1952, p. 184).

The woman, who identified herself as Mrs. Esther Albano, was taken into custody offering no resistance, actually having waited for the police. She later made a formal statement declaring that she was Mrs. Mike Pepitone, widow of the New Orleans' axman's final sacrifice. She killed Mumpre because she witnessed his foul transgressions against her sleeping husband. She had become the avenging angel come to smote the denizen of Hell!

New Orleans police discovered that Mumpre was a second rate Irish hooligan. He had both arrest and prison records. He was a burglar and gambler who sometimes cracked a few skulls. Mumpre was in New Orleans in 1911 during the attacks.

He was in jail when the attacks ceased. The attacks resumed shortly after his release in 1918. The moratorium between August 1918 and March 1919 coincided with his imprisonment for burglary. Nevertheless, he had no obvious ties with the Mafia or Black Hand. Quite the contrary, as an Irish thug he would have despised his Italian peers. If he was inclined to kill why not sleeping Italian rogues? Also, gangsters of those bygone days had a code of honor. The lives of women and children were sacred. These killings could not possibly have been "hits." He had no motive, and although violent he had no history or reputation concerning homicide. The LAPD found no incriminating evidence among his personal effects. No possible link could be forged tying him to the victims.

The only fact was that the murders did cease after Mumpre's death.

Mrs. Pepitone pleaded guilty. Public sentiment was her most valiant champion. She served forty-two months of a ten year sentence.

Even though there are many glaring holes in the Mumpre theory it did much to quiet the jangled nerves of the Crescent City's. The axman is gone. His mystery remains.

Vampires and Werewolves -

an Exposé

New Orleans is considered a mystical city. This should be no surprise to anyone acquainted with geography. Consider this: New Orleans, Cairo and Lhasa all share a common latitude—exactly 30° North. The Crescent City has been host to conspiracy theories from Napoleon's exile to the Kennedy and King assignations. It has been declared the most haunted city in America (Klein, *New Orleans Ghosts*, pp. vii, 117 for full bibliographical references of assorted authors).

Voo-Doo experienced a metamorphosis on our rich Delta soil as did the fictionalization of the Vampyr. Everything embraced by the Crescent City is forever transformed, transfixed, transcended.

New Orleans has become (since the advent of the works of Ann Rice) the epicenter for a small, but growing, dedicated coven of vampire wanna-be's. Tour guides who, before the advent of my works, were selling timeshares or hot dogs and bottled water now regularly chime on to mesmerized tourist groups about werewolves and vrykolaka (Slavic) who have existed and grown prosperous on our southern clime for generations. It is time to set the record straight.

Sources concerning Nosfara date back to the time of the Chaldean and Assyrian civilizations. Such beliefs have spread worldwide (Wright, pp. 7 & 8). Although these myths have particular strength in the Balkans and Slavic Europe (Spence, 419). The upir (Slownik) of historical legend is much different from our modern conception of a suave, urbane fiend of unbridled charm and sexuality. Such a being is usually a deceased male who preys upon the living by sucking his blood or afflicting him with a rapid degenerative disease. Respecting neither age nor sex (Summer, 1928, p. 1), it is a vile, putrefying, mindless reeking entity which is neither ghost nor demon. It is not a spirit for it has a corporeal body. The vurkulaka is best understood as an animated, malicious, murderous, mischievous monothematic corpse (Summers, 1928, p. 2). Murony (Wallachian) have the ability to shape shift and they have enormous supernatural and natural powers (Summer, 1928, p. 1) as do certain species of werewolves. Records indicate that outbreaks of Vampirism are epidemic. Each victim, at death, rises up to victimize. An arithmetic progression of exponential potential is unleashed.

There must be a first cause and that is the initial Wampira (Soruian) who through certain conditions evolved into this unpleasant state of affair. Such a person could have been guilty of a number of transgressions to merit the status of penangglan (Malaysian). Witchcraft, sorcery, suicide, excom-munication, murder, and living a particularly foul and immoral life all qualified one for the office of Wukodalak (Slavic).

Upon death such a person is baptized into the fraternity of the undead. Virtually all the seminal source material agree that such an entity is a repulsive mass of disgust   dedicated singlemindedly to human misery, terror and death.

Our modern idea of the vampyre's being a suave, compelling gentlemen of arcane lusts and passions experienced birth in a cauldron of literary activity that also produced Frankenstein's monster. Further explanation is required. On the shores of Lake Geneva a group of geniuses gathered together in 1818 for concupiscence and creativity. Lord Byron (1788-1824), Mary Wollescraft Shelley (1797-1851), Percy Shelly (1792-1851), Dr. John Polidori (1795-1821) and occasional others entertained themselves with a variety of diversions. One storm wracked night, Lord Byron suggested that they each write horror stories. Mary Shelley gave birth to *Frankenstein* or *The Modern*

Prometheus. Dr. Polidori fathered *The Vampyre.* The story's protagonist is a vampire—Lord Ruthven. The dark lord was modeled on Lord Byron and the caricature remains. The vampire had evolved from a despicable deamon to a sophisticated upper-class gentleman. It is Lord Ruthven who is father to Bram Stoker's Dracula and grandfather to Ann Rice's Lastat.

This author is well acquainted with occult source material and lore. He is also a ceremonial magician and practicing Hermeticist. Throughout my extensive researches I have never encountered any tangible trace of Vampirism in Louisiana nor New Orleans. The genesis for such beliefs is directly attributable to the commercial imagination of Ms. Rice and the cebretonic ectomorphs who, in their mad dash to establish a subjective species of identity and immortality, elevate her works to gospel status.

Now let us examine the Werewolf in the Big Easy. Werewolves, as their cousin the Vampire, are found in virtually every culture. Usually, the dominant predator of the area had the honor of melding with a person to create a fearsome hunter of human flesh. In Europe we find the werewolf. Wer is the Anglo-Saxon word for man. Wolf is old English for, obviously enough, wolf. Hence, man-wolf, werwulf. The big difference between a werwulf and vampire is that the lycanthrope is a living person. A Vampyr is essentially a reanimated corpse.

Each culture has a tradition as to the origin of this manifestation. For our limited purpose we will examine the legend coming from Arcadia, an ancient pastoral region in the Peloponnesus. It is also a word which has come to mean any region of rustic simplicity. Arcadia is often used in reference to southern Louisiana and the Cajun people who live there. So this is a very appropriate myth.

Pausanias writing circa 170 C.E. speaks of a great king of the region living before the Greek classical period after the founding of Athens by Cecrops.

The regent was Lycaon. He was an ambitious and resourceful ruler. Lycaon built a fabulous city, Lycosura, on an extinct volcano Mount Lycacus. It was at his city, Lycosura that the Lucaean games were begun. As a final show of his influence he gave the great god Zeus the surname Lycaean.

Lycaon, in his mad dash to gain favor with the deity, began sacrificing newborn babies to the King of Gods. His efforts had the opposite effect. Zeus recoiled in disgust and immediately transformed our overzealous prince into a ravaging wolf. From this history we have inherited the word Lycanthropy which designates werewolfism (Gould, p. 13; Summers, 1933, pp. 133ff).

In Western civilization this manifestation was especially pronounced in France, accounting for its presence in Louisiana. From this Latin influence many *truisms* were voiced and given imprimatur. A shape shifter could be either voluntary or involuntary. If voluntary, the metamorphosis was determined by will and ritual. Such an occurrence was part of the domain of Magick, and as such was contingent upon human desire and will.

This author, apart from being a folklorist and historian, is also a practicing occultist and ritual Magus. As such I feel it is appropriate to include a *Werwolf* ritual in the text for the enlightenment and entertainment of the reader; however, I must voice a caveat. Many occult rituals require dangerous or illegal chemicals and drugs. Since this is the case it is incumbent upon the author to say that this ritual is only printed here for its historic interest and not intended nor recommended for actual shape-shifting experiments. Also, occult rituals should be avoided by all except initiated Magi because they can cause extreme psychological dislocations.

During the first full moon of autumn at midnight repair to a forest clearing. The aspirant will then trace two concentric circles on the ground: one six feet and the other twelve feet in diameter. In the center of the inner circle build a fire. Suspend from an iron tripod an iron pot filled with water from a flowing stream. As the water boils the Magus throws a handful each of aloe, belladonna, hemlock, poppy seed and deadly nightshade into the cauldron.

While the liquid again reaches the boiling point the would-be shape shifter disrobes completely and rubs a salve over her naked body. The salve is composed of the fat of a freshly killed sheep or goat mixed with anise, camphor, nutmeg and opium (approximately one ounce of each). After the body is covered with the salve the aspirant should wrap a length of wolf skin around her waist, kneel and begin to visualize the Astral Body of Rage which confers this frightening gift. Immediately after this visualization exercise she should say aloud and with great passion and conviction the following lines:

Hail, Hail, Hail, great wolf spirit, Hail!
A boon I ask thee, mighty shade.
Within this circle I have made.
Make me a werewolf strong and bold.
The terror alike of young and old.
Grant me a figure tall and spare;
The speed of the elk, the claws of the bear;
The poison of snakes, the wit of the fox;
The stealth of the wolf, the strength of the ox;
The jaws of the tiger, the teeth of the shark;
The eyes of a cat that sees in the dark;
Make me climb like a monkey, scent like a dog;
Swim like a fish, and eat like a hog.
Hate, Haste, Haste, Lonely spirit, Haste!
Here, wan and drear, magic spell making,
Findest thou - shaking, quaking.
Softly fan me as I lie.
And thy mystic touch apply.
Touch apply, and I swear that when I die,
When I die, I will serve thee evermore,
Evermore, in grey wolf land, cold and raw.
The incantation concluded, the supplicant then kisses the ground three times, and advances to the fire, takes off the iron vessel, and whirling it smoking round his head, cries out;
Make me a werewolf! Make me a Man-hunter!
Make me a werewolf! Make me a Man-hunter!
Make me a werewolf! Make me a Man-hunter!
I pine for blood! Blood! Human
Give it to me! Give it to me tonight!
Great Wolf Spirit! Give it to me, and heart, body, and soul,
I am yours.

If the ritual is successful a dark entity will be made manifest accompanied by wind, screams and an ineffable growling. The form will continue to gain substance until the sorceress is confronted by a huge, half wolf half human abomination of fantastic size and power. After the manifestation is complete the witch may begin her negotiations in order to be granted the dark power of transformation.

Again, I emphasize that this procedure is reproduced here only for historical interest and on no account should it be practiced.

Involuntary werewolves are afflicted in much the same manner as their cousin - the vampire. Being bitten or scratched by an existing werewolf does the trick. Also various and sundry affronts to established religion is another vehicle to deliver the curse.

Now for the werewolf in Louisiana. Apart from the legends of Native Americans, traditions of Vampires and Werewolves are basically absent from European-American mythology. The general exception to the reality is the belief in the Loup-Garous (pronounced Roo-Ga-Roo) by Cajuns and the Creole Afro-American populations of southern Louisiana (Saxon, 191).

There are many "loup-garous," some, people under a spell, and others enjoying self-imposed enchantment. A Cajun will explain: "Loup-garous is them people what wants to do bad work, and changes themselves into wolves. They got plenty of them, yes. And you sure know them when you see them. They got big red eyes, pointed noses and everything just like a wolf has, even hair all over, and long pointed nails. They rub themselves with some Voo-Doo grease and come out just like wolves is. You keep away you see any of them things, hein? They make you one of them, yes, quick like hell. They hold balls on Bayou Goula all the time, mens and womens, both together. They dance and carry on just like animals, them. If you see one, you just get yourself one nice frog and throw him at them things. They sure gon' run then. They scared of frogs. That's the only way to chase a 'loup-garou' away from you.. Bullets go right through him."

"Loup-garous" have bats as big as airplanes to carry them where they want to go. They make these bats drop them down your chimney, and they stand by your bed and say, "I got you now, me!" Then they bite you and suck your blood and that makes you a "loup-garou," and soon you

find yourself dancing at their balls at Bayou Goula and
carrying on just as they do. You're a lost soul.
'Is a good idea to hang a new sifter outside from your
house, yes. Then they got to stop and count every hole in
that sifter, and you catch them and sprinkle them with salt.
That sets them on fire and they step out of them shaggy
old skins and runs away. But me, I don't fool "round with
no loup-garous!" (Saxon, p. 191)

Fascinated by the bizarre and unusual all of his life, this
author came across an article in the local paper, *The Times-Picayune* sometime in 1983 or '84. It was from a wire service,
AP or UPI. Cutting it out, I subsequently lost it. I have tried to
resurface the story to no avail. The closest I've come is a citing
on the Internet included in the appendix and listed as (from the
files of G.C.B.R.O., Appendix D).

Notwithstanding I shall relate the story as I remember it in the
hope that some other researcher will have better luck than me
in finding the original source material. When someone does
surface these data I would appreciate his sending it to me at the
address listed in this present work so that I may preserve it is
my private files.

Caddo Parish, Louisiana, is a rural district in the Northwest
corner of the state. The news release I read stated that on
several occasions residents of this bucolic area had observed
a large, bipedal, canine-like creature with incandescent eyes.
Whatever it was, was very aggressive in that it killed quite a
number of livestock and left its footprints under the windows of
several houses. The state police were alerted and managed to
preserve several footprints in plaster. These specimens were
forwarded to Louisiana State University Baton Rouge where
they were examined by zoologists. Their reported findings were
cryptic at best. Essentially, they found that the tracks were too
ambiguous to provide a clear identity for the beast although it
bore unmistakable canine characteristics.

I contacted the state police only to be confronted with
expected ignorance and evasion. My next step was contacting
the reporter who presented the story. He was intrigued by my
interest, and wanted to believe I was more than just a curious
researcher of arcane lore. He gave me scant information that
was not in his story.

Now, for a little something one won't find in the inanity of the fiction writers–Truth. The existence of these monsters can also be attributed to two possibilities never imagined by the *so called* writers who, like the fictional vampires they create, live off the blood of an uninitiated and foolish public.

The first is an existential reality of as yet undefined dimensions. Because of our awareness of our own impending deaths we descend into the murky depths of religions promising immortality–of course, we must be dead in order to gain this absurd promise. St. Clair and Brophy, two anthropologists, put forth the idea that vampires and their ilk are actually the result of a soul's rebellion against the inevitable reality of physical death (Gould, p. 105).

Edgar Allen Poe mirrors this in Ligeia:

. . . *Who—who knoweth the mysteries of the will with its vigor? Man doth not yield him to the angels, nor unto death utterly, save only through the weakness of his feeble will.*

Another concept of equal interest is the realm of astral beings. In this alleged extra-dimensional sphere of being it is theorized that among its denizens are non-integrated aspects of psychology.   Human psychology is made up of many emotions–love, fear, faith, anger, elation, lust, admiration, rage and so on. The astral theory proposes that each of these emotions exist as an unintegrated, unique manifestation completely sovereign unto itself. Through some mechanism: ritual, will, a curse, et al., this projection can manifest itself in a human being with magnificent results, i.e. shape shifting accompanied with monolithic, monothematic Rage!

Herbert Spencer (1820-1903) maintained that all myths and legends have some basis in fact. Historical records across the globe are littered with eldritch accounts of the undead and shape shifters.   Much can be dismissed on account of ignorance, superstition and hysteria. There exist among us those who know much more than is revealed. On this note I leave the reader.

Epilogue

Death is the unique mystery facing humanity. Death and sex are the only experiences held in common by humans regardless of the chance categories of culture, sex, race, age, et al. Death transcends and equalizes all. It is also the genesis of religion—after all, religion is ultimately a death denial exercise.

Best of all, of course, religion solves the problem of death, which no living individuals can solve, no matter how they would support us. Religion, then, gives the possibility of heroic victory in freedom and solves the problem of human dignity at its highest level. The two ontological motives of the human condition are both met: the need to surrender oneself in full to the rest of nature, to become a part of it by laying down one's whole existence to some higher meaning; and the need to expand oneself as an individual heroic personality. Finally, religion alone gives hope, because it holds open the dimension of the unknown and the unknowable, the fantastic mystery of creation that the human mind cannot even begin to approach, the possibility of a multidimensionality of spheres of existence, of

*heavens and possible embodiments that make
a mockery of earthly logic—and in doing so, it
relieves the absurdity of earthly life, all the
impossible limitations and frustrations of living
matter. In religious terms, to "see God" is to die,
because the creature is too small and finite to be
able to bear the higher meanings of creation.
Religion takes one's very creatureliness, one's
insignificance, and makes it a condition of hope.
Full transcendence of the human condition
means limitless possibility unimaginable to us.
(Becker, 1973, pp. 203-4)*

Every culture has speculated about this final episode.
Anthropological evidence informs us that our paleolithic
ancestors practiced elaborate funerary procedures for their
dead which included placing the deceased in fetal positions in
prepared graves; covering the corpse in cinnabar, and
surrounding it with flowers, herbs and talismans. Such
ritualized, final farewells are a hallmark of the human condition.

Concomitantly, all cultures display traditions concerning a
species of the afterlife that can be summed by the word *ghost*.
Since this work is directed to a Western readership primarily it
is informative to investigate briefly how the predominant
Western religion views this peculiar manifestation.

Since Martin Luther (1483-1546), Western Christianity has
been fragmented permanently into two camps: Catholic and
Protestant. Speaking basically, the Catholic explanation of
ghosts is easier to explain because its articulation of this
phenomenon flows from a unified, centralized voice. Ghosts
(the appearance of the dead to the living) can be enumerated as
one of two events:

1. Supernatural
2. Natural

The supernatural scenario is exemplified by such
occurrences as the various appearances of the Virgin Mary.
Such events are allowed by God in order to reinforce faith.
They also act as vehicles to communicate God's will.

Natural causes result from a need on the part of the
deceased to address an injustice. A good example of this would
be the alleged haunting of the Tower of London by Ann Boleyn

(1507-36) the hapless second wife of Henry VIII (1491-1547). The theological justification of this type of natural haunting is that God allows such in order that those who witness it will be inspired to pray for these spiritual bodies existing in time so that such entities, through the intercession of prayer, may find reconciliation.

A final explanation is that such events are the product of a disturbed mind. No doubt psychopathology has played a big part in the creation of ghosts and their kin (interview with Father Val McInnis, O.P., 8 November 1999).

The Protestant position on ghosts is an either/or proposition. Either ghosts don't exist and such beliefs are pure foolishness, or their existence is a manifestation of demonic influence. Since the Protestants did away with Purgatory these souls have been relegated to the sovereignty of the Dark Prince. Conservative, evangelical Protestantism is infamous for its adversarial *us against them* intolerant attitude toward any phenomena or activity that does not fit into their theocratic agenda of repression and hypocrisy

This universe is much more complex than we can ever imagine. To deny mystery on the basis of ignorance or fear is to deny the very thing that articulates our humanity—our ability to transcend mystery through critical reflection. A salient purpose of these anthropologically significant works on ghosts is to encourage the reader to approach the unknown (not just simply ghosts) with a spirit of optimism and curiosity based on the firm conviction that humanity, through its own agencies, will one day transcend the fetters of ignorance and superstition and look upon itself not as the fearful servants of an ill-imagined and erroneously conceived deity, but as co-operators and co-sustainers of a universe in which it is a conscious, eternal component.

Appendix A

Patrick Larrieu displays documents he says support his claim to parts of City Park.   JACKSON CITIZEN PATRIOT PHOTO

City Park accused of shady land deal

By GREGORY ROBERTS
Staff·writer

Patrick Larrieu has a straight-forward objective: He simply wants it recognized that his family owns City Park.

Well, not all of City Park. But a good chunk of it, including the land occupied by the New Orleans Museum of Art, Tad Gormley Stadium and Roosevelt Mall.

Larrieu acknowledges it's unrealistic to expect the return of the City Park land and other parcels he said were stripped from his great-grandmother and her children. But he would like suitable commemoration of his family's role in the park's history, maybe in a plaque near the main entrance. And he also would like financial satisfaction, with current fair market value as a starting point. That, he said, could run into the billions.

"We want restitution and compensation," Larrieu said from his home in Michigan last week. "We want to work it out fairly and

Roosevelt Mall is part of the land that Patrick Larrieu wants compensation for.

amenably for everyone. It's just a good, common-sense approach to a disastrous situation."

City Park executive director Beau Bassich offers a different perspective on Larrieu's claim. "We just don't see anything in it," he said last week.

See CITY PARK, next page

Bassich's file on Larrieu includes statements from park lawyers who have concluded that the Larrieu land was obtained legitimately. The file also includes a 1990 note to then-City Attorney Okla Jones on Larrieu's allegations. "If he keeps this up," Bassich wrote to Jones, "he may claim all of the city."

It's a story with the earmarks of a classic Louisiana succession case: death and remarriage, community property, an unsigned will, minor heirs, a tangled web of petitions and court judgments, a moldering pile of handwritten documents in French and English. Larrieu's fascination with it goes back a half-dozen years.

Larrieu, 50 and self-employed in insurance and finance, grew up in a firefighter's family on Joseph Street and attended De La Salle High School before leaving New Orleans. It was on a visit to relatives in the city that he first got caught up in the case.

"My sister and I were just chit-chatting with my wife and children," he said. "We just became inquisitive. We primarily wanted to find out where we were from. All of a sudden, everything started unraveling."

The story winds back to Auguste Larrieu, a native of France who emigrated to New Orleans after the Civil War. Larrieu acquired a coffee stand in the French Market and another in the old public market on Poydras Street. But his main enterprise was a dairy farm with more than 100 cows on about 200 acres of scrub brush, willow stands and dried-out marsh he owned along Bayou St. John and Metairie Road, now known as City Park Avenue. For a time, Larrieu's Ville de Londres dairy held the contract to furnish milk to Charity Hospital.

Larrieu married a woman named Mary Clark in New Orleans and the couple had four children: Auguste in 1876, Mary in 1877, James in 1878 and Henriette in 1879. But Larrieu did not live to see them grow up. In 1890, at 38, he fell ill, and at 8:30 p.m. on March 14, he died in his three-bedroom house overlooking the bayou.

A few hours before his death, Larrieu had summoned notary public Charles Theard to his bedside to record the dictation of his last will and testament. According to the handwritten document filed in French by Theard, Larrieu bequeathed to his wife the life use of all his property and named as executor his friend, Hippolyte Borey.

But there was a glitch in the process. "When it was time to sign," Theard wrote, "the testator declared to the notary, in the presence of the witnesses, that he

was too weak to sign; for this reason, this instrument was not signed by the testator."

The will was accepted by the courts. The estate was valued near $20,000.

In accordance with Louisiana inheritance law at the time, a half-interest in Larrieu's property went to the widow and a half-interest to the children jointly. In 1897, according to City Park attorneys, Larrieu's widow sold part of the Bayou St. John land to the adjoining park, with her children signing off on the sale and declaring their interest in the entire parcel was erased. In 1903, she sold the last 180 acres of her Bayou St. John land to a real-estate developer, with the park acquiring the property in 1920, according to the 1982 book "Historic City Park, New Orleans," written by Sally K. Evans Reeves and others and published by the Friends of City Park.

Meanwhile, Auguste Larrieu's son, Auguste, went into the insurance business, married and raised a son named Lloyd Paul Larrieu, who eventually joined the New Orleans Fire Department, moved into a house on Joseph Street and raised his own family, including Patrick.

Patrick Larrieu's plaint begins with his great-grandfather's will, the one that wasn't signed. "It's a worthless piece of paper," he said. "You do not probate an instrument which has no signature on it. It's just legally impossible."

Larrieu said the courts should have ruled that his great-grandfather died intestate — without leaving a will. If that were the case, he said, disposition of the estate would have been deter-

mined by the provisions of an international treaty between France and the United States, because Auguste Larrieu was a French national. And that would have meant protection of the estate on behalf of the children.

But instead, he said, "They took advantage of that woman and her children."

To right the wrong as he sees it, Larrieu has spent countless hours digging through old records and deeds. He has amassed 35 pounds of documents. He has made numerous trips to New Orleans. He has spent a lot of money.

He has no regrets. And he thinks victory is near.

But like any good inheritance story, this one has a touch of irony.

In a 1991 letter to Larrieu, City Park lawyer Robert Steeg declared "the public records indicate to us there is no legal or factual basis to your claims that the transfers from your ancestors are not valid." And if it should turn out they weren't valid, Steeg said, the park would be in a position to sue whomever it purchased the land from, who could sue whomever they purchased it from, and so on.

"If your claims have validity, your recourse is not against City Park, but against your relatives," Steeg said. "In fact, it may turn out that you have liability."

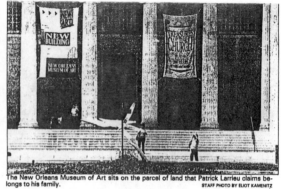

The New Orleans Museum of Art sits on the parcel of land that Patrick Larrieu claims belongs to his family.
STAFF PHOTO BY ELIOT KAMENITZ

A woman strolls along a picturesque lagoon in City Park.

Larrieu dairy at City Park

TP 9/8/91

New Orleans

Re the Lagniappe article on Aug. 30 titled "A Century in the Park" by Constance Snow:

There seems to be a sizable gap in the history of City Park which, unfortunately, very few people know about. This lapse involves my family's dairy which comprised more than 200 acres in what is now City Park.

The boundaries of the large tract extended from Metairie Road (now City Park Avenue) to Taylor Drive, and from Bayou St. John to Orleans Avenue. This property was not only where my family resided but also from where Auguste Larrieu, a native of France, conducted his business operations.

The Larrieu home, a two-story Creole cottage, was situated where the bayou meets Esplanade Avenue (present-day entrance to City Park). Records even show that my great-grandfather, Auguste, beautified his land with many trees.

The article referred to "long stretches of barbed wire to discourage roaming cattle from the surrounding dairy farms." My family's dairy was more than a few "roaming cows" into a small undeveloped park at the time. In fact, these "roaming cattle" were the basis for a thriving and prosperous business enterprise in New Orleans started by Auguste Larrieu in the 1870s.

He purchased the land (now City Park) in early 1889 and died the following year at age 38 as a result of an accident on his dairy. His surviving wife with her four young children, including my grandfather Auguste, operated the dairy until 1903 when they no longer had possession of the land.

The Larrieu dairy business made great contributions to this city, as did many other dairies in the City Park area; a contribution much more important than some "roaming cattle." Augustine's dairy provided jobs, both directly and indirectly, to this city — an industry New Orleans could only wish for today.

Hopefully, this brief account of the Larrieu dairy will fill an important and unexplained gap in the history of City Park. Without it, the entire and true story of City Park's formation from Allard to present-day is incomplete.

Noelie Larrieu Wright

Appendix B

COME VISIT THE NEW ORLEANS PHARMACY MUSEUM & LEARN MORE ABOUT VOODOO, GRIS-GRIS & PHARMACY

THE VOODOO DANCE.

From an engraving by E. W. Kemble, 1886, "Dance and Song of Voodoo Worship". Vodou was widely practiced in New Orleans throughout the 19th century. The Sunday dances of the slaves in Congo Square, just blocks away from Dufilho's Apothecary Shop were legalized by the Municipal Council in 1817.

NEW ORLEANS PHARMACY MUSEUM · EST 1823 ·

"Gris-Gris" potions could be obtained from the Vodou Priestess or the local pharmacist. These "formulas" written by a New Orleans Pharmacist, c.1900 are from the collections of the New Orleans Pharmacy Museum.

514 rue Chartres - New Orleans, La. 70130 - (504) 565-8027 - Fax (504) 565-8028

"Gris-Gris"

In many African languages, a single term (pidgin English -- "ju-ju"; colonial French -- "gris-gris") is used to refer to magical objects and complex magical processes (roots, remedies and rituals) having curative and protective powers and to pharmaceutical preparations associated with healing. In the practice of Voodoo medicine there is no distinction between curative magic and drugs.

Magical acts and ritual activities vary greatly, from the simple recitation of a ready-made formula, which is similar to prayer, to the making of amulets and talismans and are referred to as "gris-gris" within the practice of Voodoo -- a Yoruba religion. Magic and technical skill are inseparable and form an effective combination.

HIGH JOHN THE CONQUEROR ROOT
(Ipomoea Purga or I. Jalapa)

Gender: Masculine
Planet: Mars
Element: Fire
Powers: Money, Love, Success, Happiness

Magical Uses: Anoint one of the roots with mint oil and tie up in a green sachet. Carry to attract money. John the Conqueror is also carried to stop depression, bring love and success, protect from all hexes and curses, and to break and destroy spells and hexes.

To make a simple anointing oil suitable for all purposes, take three (3) High John the conqueror roots, make small cuts into them with a sharp knife, and place these in a bottle of vegetable, olive oil or mineral oil. Let the roots soak in the oil for several weeks. Leave the roots in the oil and used as desired: to anoint candles, sachets, etc.

History: In 1574, Nicholas Monardes, a wealthy Seville doctor with a modest fashionable practice and an enthusiast for new drugs wrote that jalap (Ipomoea purga) from Mexico was a most effective new purgative. Louis XIV's physician and Dr. Benjamin Rush agreed, combining jalap with calomel.

Folklore: Considered one of the most powerful "gris-gris" in voodoo medicine. "High John the Conqueror" was also worn around the neck to prevent yellow fever, cholera, and malaria. Mississippi riverboat gamblers rubbed the roots for luck before dealing their cards or rolling the dice.

"La Pharmacie Francaise" New Orleans Pharmacy Museum
514 rue Chartres
New Orleans, Louisiana USA
(504) 565-8027

19TH CENTURY PATENT MEDICINES:
MIRACLES CURES & REMEDIES

During Patent Medicine's heyday – from the 1870's to the 1930's – remedies like Lydia E. Pinkham's Vegetable Compound, Hostetter's Celebrated Stomach Bitters, Coca-Cola and Moxie were as much a part of the American household medicine cabinet as aspirin is today.

Most 19th century American patent medicines were not actually patented, referring to royal patents granted by European royalty to their favorite medicine makers. If they were patented, medicine makers would have to disclose their secret formulas. The secret to the success of these proprietary medicines was the secrecy of their formulas.

"SODA FOUNTAINS – AN AMERICAN PHENOMENON"

Soda fountains were introduced in American pharmacies in the 1830's as a way of dispensing medications – a little flavoring and a little seltzer in your medicine to make it more palatable. Our Italian black and rose marble soda fountain dates 1855. Mineral and seltzers were dispensed from the top brass faucets, fruit nectars and phosphate flavorings from the bottom. The brass plate reads "Chas. Lippincott, Philadelphia." Pharmacists claimed they made medicines taste so good, people wanted them, whether they needed them or not, and that's how soft drinks evolved. The American Pharmacist increasingly became a merchant and dispenser of medicines, a specialist in confections, fancy elixirs, fruit nectars, phosphate sodas, and invigorating rejuvenating tonics.

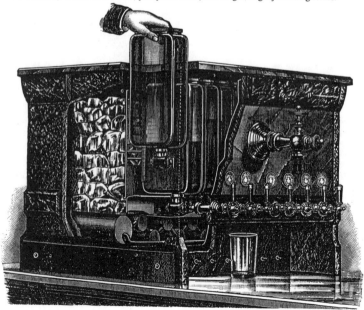

THE IDEAL BRAIN TONIC – COCA COLA

The original Coca-Cola, created in 1886 by Atlanta pharmacist Dr. John Pemberton, contained carbonated water, cane sugar syrup, caffeine, and extracts of kola nuts and coca leaves. It was advertised as a "brain tonic and intellectual beverage" that was also supposed to ease menstrual distress. In 1893, responding to growing concerns over the dangers of cocaine, the amount of coca in the drink was reduced to a trace. A candy storeowner in Vicksburg, Mississippi was the first to bottle the drink in 1894. It had previously been sold only at soda fountains. By 1895, the drink was sold in all U.S. states and territories. Today, the world's hottest selling soft drink is flavored with a non-narcotic extract of coca, the plant from which cocaine is made.

"YOU'VE GOT A LOT OF MOXIE"

Moxie, a new England based soft drink once as popular as Coca-Cola, was also originally a patent medicine. Known as "beverage Moxie Nerve Food", its label promised to cure "brain and nervous exhaustion, loss of manhood, imbecility and helplessness, softening of the brain, locomotor ataxia and insanity."

"IT TAKES THE OUCH OUT OF GROUCH"

In October, 1929, before the stock market crash, St. Louis businessman, Charles L. Grigg began marketing a beverage called "Bib-Label Lithiated Lemon Lime Soda". His slogan: "Takes the 'ouch' out of grouch". The name was later changed to "7 UP", the "7" stood for its 7 oz. Bottle, the "UP" for the bubbles rising from its heavy carbonation (later reduced). The lithium was listed on the label until the mid 1940's. Identified chemically in 1817, lithium was prescribed for gout, uremia, kidney stones and rheumatism, for which it does little good, worse it can harm heart and kidney patients. Lithium, a powerful drug, is now prescribed for manic-depressives.

COCKTAILS & PHARMACY

An early contribution to American social life was made in the late 18th century by the New Orleans Pharmacist Antoine Peychaud, who dispensed tonics of cognac mixed with his own Peychaud bitters. This mixture – which was served in an eggcup (French coquetier) – was the forerunner, etymologically as well as actually, of the "cocktail". A before dinner drink served by the pharmacist to gentlemen only.

A. A. Peychaud was listed in the New Orleans City Directory on Royal Street from 1841 –1867.

New Orleans Pharmacy Museum. 514 rue Chartres, New Orleans, Louisiana. 70130-2110.
Telephone: (504) 565-8027   Fax: (504) 565-8028.

Value of Herbs

AJUGA - - *stops hemorrhage*
similar to digitalis

ANISE - - *for indigestion*

BAY LEAF - - *helps sprains*

CALENDULA - - *relieves heart pain,*
good for spirit

CAMOMILE - - *headache and neuralgia*

CHRYSANTHEMUM - - *hysteria, nerves*

DILL - - *for soothing sleep*

LAVENDER - - *makes wash white*

MARJORAM - - *convulsions*

OREGANO - - *reduces rheumatic swelling*

PEPPERMINT TEA - - *for nausea*

PARSLEY - - *removes smell of garlic*

ROSEMARY - - *is a disinfectant*

RUE - - *for vision*

SHALLOT - - *for strength*

SAGE - - *helps nerves, puts fever to flight*

VIOLETS - - *skin disorders, roots used*
as a purgative.

SISTER XAVIER, O.S.U.
1st woman pharmacist in U.S.A.
Old Ursuline Convent

FRANCO FÊTE '99
le tricentenaire de la Louisiane

Appendix C

From the files of
(G.C.B.R.O.)

Submitted by Bobby Hamilton. Reported by Confidential

REPORT RECEIVED: From the G.C.B.R.O. Web Site Submission Form

DATE: Summer 1984

TIME: Not Given

LOCATION: Caddo Parish, Louisiana

TERRAIN: Wooded

OBSERVED: I was just a young kid then, but I used to go to a summer camp every summer near Caddo Lake. What happened was i was playing with some other kids, near a wooded area, and one of them said "LOOK", I looked and saw a face looking at us thru some thick brush. I thad both hands on either side of its face holding apart a path for it to view us. It quickly leaned back and let the branches go, and that was the last we saw of it. None of us seemed to fear the thing. I mean we didn't get any feelings of being in any danger or anything. But what I saw in the 2-3 seconds I viewed it before it left, was that it had a big head, was lite brownish in color, had big dark hollow looking eyes, a large broad nose, not a flat nose, but broad. It was probably about 7-8 foot off the ground and it seemed to have a look of curiousity on its face. That is really all there was too it.

Activities of Witness:

Description of Creature: Large head, brownish color, dark hollow eyes and broad nose. It was about 7-8 foot tall.

Other Notes:

Acknowledgements

Tulane University, Louisiana Collection, for valuable research
assistance and Ken Owen and Dr. Wilbur Meneray

La Pharmacie Française and Museum Director Liz Good for
permission to use documents in Appendix B

LSUBR which conferred the MLS degree upon the author
opening the world of bibliographic research

Marianne Mason Morrison for her practiced editorial eye

Barbara Mulé for her encouragement and dedicated, patient
word-processing

Bibliography

Askew, Teresa. "Fleur List: New Orleans Top Haunted House Legends." *New Orleans Magazine*, October 1989, p. 16.

Becker, Ernst. *The Denial of Death*, New York: The Free Press, 1973.

Baring-Gould, Sabine. *The Book of Werewolves*, New York: Causeway Books, 1973. (First pub. 1865)

Conrad, Glenn R. *A Dictionary of Louisiana Biography*, ed. , Lafayette, Louisiana: Published by The Louisiana Association in cooperation with The Center for Louisiana Studies of the University of Southwestern Louisiana, 1988.

Conrad, Glenn R. (Ed.). *The Cajuns: Essays on Their History and Culture.* Lafayette, Louisiana: Center for Louisiana Studies, University of Southwestern Louisiana, 1978.

Cowan, Walter G., et al. New Orleans: *Yesterday and Today,* 1st ed. Baton Rouge, LA: Louisiana Shale University Press, 1983.

deLavigne, Jeanne. *Ghost Stores of Old New Orleans*, New York, New York: Rinehart and Co., Inc., 1946.

Fox, F. G. *Bizarre New Orleans,* New Orleans: St. Expedite Press, 1997.

Garvey, John B. and Mary Lou Garvey. *Beautiful Crescent: A History of New Orleans*, 3rd ed., New Orleans: Garmor Press, Inc., 1984.

Gurtner, Gange. "Looking for New Haunts—Larry Montz, Ghostbuster." *New Orleans Magazine*, October 1996, pp. 115-116.

Hunted History "New Orleans." *The Times-Picayune.*

Huber, Leonard V. *New Orleans: A Pictorial History,* New York: Crown Publishers, Inc., 1971.

Klein, Victor C. *New Orleans Ghosts,* Metairie, LA: Lycanthrope Press, 1996.

Keith, Don Lee. "Some Call It Haunted." *New Orleans Magazine*, October 1991, p. 119.

Laborde, Errol. *New Orleans Magazine,* October 1980, pp. 79-88.

Several references were through interviews cited in the text by the person's name and relationship to the site. These interviews have been recorded and are ensconced in the author's private files. Also, newspaper references are listed in the text as title of paper and date.

Mascetti, Manuela Dunn. *Vampire: The Complete Guide to the World of the Undead*, New York: Viking Penguin, 1992.

Melton, J. Gordon. *The Vampire Book: The Encyclopedia of the Undead*, Detroit, MI: Viking Ink Press, 1994.

Myers, Arthur. *The Ghostly Register*, New York: Contemporary Books, Inc.

Port of New Orleans. "Brochure," P. O. Box 60046m, New Orleans, LA 70160. (504) 522-2551; (504) 524-4156 FAX.

Rose, Christopher, "Mourning Glories." *Times-Picayune,* Sunday, October 27, 1996, D4-D6.

Ryan, Thomas, Henry. Historical Souvenir–New Orleans City Park, on the Occasion of the Fourth Grand Festival and Fete Champetre, under the Auspices of the New Orleans City Park Improvement Association, Sunday and Monday.

Saxon, Lyle, & Robert Tallant. *Gumbo Va -Va.* Louisiana Writers Project Publishers, 3rd series. Cambridge, MA: The Riverside Press, 1945.

Smith, Katherine. *Journey into Darkness*, New Orleans, LA: De Simonin Publications, 1998.

Spence, Lewis. *An Encyclopedia of Occultism*, New Hyde Park, New York: University Books, 1960. (First pub. 1933)

Stanforth, Deirdue, et al. *Romantic New Orleans*, New York: The Viking Press, 1977.

Staff, et al., "Ghost Writers." *Times-Picayune,* Sunday, October 27, 1996, D1 and D4-5.

Summers, Montague. *The Vampire: His Kith and Kin*, New York: University Books, 1960. (First pub. 1928)

Summers, Montague. *The Werewolf*, Syracuse, NJ: University Books, Inc., 1960. (First pub. 1933)

Tallant, Robert. "Ready to Hang." *Seven Famous Murders in New Orleans.* "The Axeman Wore Wings," New York: Harper & Brothers, 1952.

Tallant, Robert. *Murder in New Orleans: Seven Famous Trials.* London: William Kimber, 1953.

Taylor, John Gray. *Louisiana A Bicentennial History,* New York: W. W. Norton and Company, 1976.

Wellborn, Alfred. History of New Orleans City Park. Thirty-Fifth Annual Report, New Orleans City Park Improvement Assn., 1926.

Wilson, Colin, etc. *The Killers Among Us*. New York: Wanage Books, 1995.

Wright, Dudley. *The Book of Vampires*, New York: Causeway Books, 1973. (First pub. 1914)

INDEX

To order additional copies of any of Victor C. Klein works, please complete the order form below:

New Orleans Ghosts II $12.00
New Orleans Ghosts 12.00
Soul Shadows 12.00
Hermes and Christ 20.00
My Motto Is 6.00
A Poor Store 100.00
Academic Papers X Vols. 2,000.00

Order Form

Name_____

Street Address_____

City_____State_____

Zip Code_____Daytime phone_____

e-mail address_____

TITLE	Quantity	PRICE	TOTAL

TOTAL . . . . _____

Price includes postage and handling. **Same Day Shipping.**

Money Orders <u>only</u> payable to:
　　　　Ordo Templi Veritatis
　　　　Post Office Box 9028
　　　　Metairie, LA   70005-9028